DAILY READINGS FROM
EVERY DAY A FRIDAY

ALSO BY JOEL OSTEEN

Every Day a Friday
Your Best Life Now
Become a Better You
It's Your Time

Available from FaithWords wherever books are sold.

DAILY READINGS FROM
EVERY DAY A FRIDAY

90 DEVOTIONS TO BE HAPPIER 7 DAYS A WEEK

JOEL OSTEEN

Faith Words

New York   Boston   Nashville

Scripture quotations noted AMP are from *The Amplified Bible.* Copyright © 1954, 1958, 1962, 1964, 1965, 1987 by The Lockman Foundation. All rights reserved.
Used by permission. (www.Lockman.org)
Scripture quotations noted ESV are from The Holy Bible, English Standard Version, © 2001 by Crossway Bibles, a publishing ministry of Good News Publishers.
Used by permission. All rights reserved.
Scripture quotations noted KJV are from the King James Version of the Holy Bible.
Scripture quotations noted NIV are from The Holy Bible, New International Version® NIV®. Copyright © 1973, 1978, 1984, 2011 by Biblica, Inc. ™.
Used by permission. All rights reserved worldwide.
Scripture quotations noted NKJV are from the New King James Version.
Copyright © 1979, 1980, 1982, Thomas Nelson, Inc., Publishers.
Scripture quotations noted NLT are from the *Holy Bible*, New Living Translation, copyright © 1996, 2004. Used by permission of Tyndale House Publishers, Inc., Wheaton, Illinois 60189. All rights reserved.
Scripture quotations noted THE MESSAGE are taken from *The Message.*
Copyright © 1993, 1994, 1995, 1996, 2000, 2001, 2002.
Used by permission of NavPress Publishing Group.
Portions of this book have been adapted from *Every Day a Friday.* Copyright © 2011 by Joel Osteen. Published by FaithWords, a division of Hachette Book Group, Inc.

FaithWords
Hachette Book Group
237 Park Avenue
New York, NY 10017
www.faithwords.com

Printed in the United States of America

RRD-C

First Edition: November 2012

10 9 8 7 6 5 4 3 2 1

FaithWords is a division of Hachette Book Group, Inc.
The FaithWords name and logo are trademarks of Hachette Book Group, Inc.

The Hachette Speakers Bureau provides a wide range of authors for speaking events. To find out more, go to www.hachettespeakersbureau.com or call (866) 376-6591.

The publisher is not responsible for websites (or their content) that are not owned by the publisher.

Library of Congress Cataloging-in-Publication Data

Osteen, Joel.
Daily readings from every day a Friday / Joel Osteen.
p. cm.
ISBN 978-0-89296-992-0 — ISBN 978-1-4555-2265-1 (large print) 1. Happiness—Religious aspects—Christianity—Meditations. 2. Joy—Religious aspects—Christianity—Meditations.
I. Osteen, Joel. Every day a Friday. II. Title.
BV4647.J68O87 2012
242'.2—dc23
                                                              2012008307

CONTENTS

PART I
Don't Give Away Your Power

PART II
Know What to Ignore

PART III
Live Without Crutches

PART IV
Travel Light

PART V
Laugh Often

PART VI
Be a Dream Releaser

PART VII

Celebrate Yourself

INTRODUCTION

I wrote *Every Day a Friday* after reading about a number of studies related to the positive effects of happiness. One showed that people are happier on Fridays. Another showed that Mondays are so stressful for some that more heart attacks occur on that day than others. There were also a number of reports about the positive impact of happiness and optimism on mental and physical health.

After reading all this research, I wanted to encourage people to see every day of the week as a gift from God, and to live each day with gratitude, good humor, and faith. *Daily Readings from **Every Day a Friday*** is designed to help you do just that, one day at a time.

This collection of ninety daily devotionals contains excerpts from the original book that emphasize positive, inspiring, and faith-building messages, along with additional supportive and encouraging material in the form of key Bible verses, daily prayers, and daily thoughts.

I hope my words and the other material in this daily devotional will lift your spirits, ignite your faith, and increase God's favor in your life.

*Daily Readings from **Every Day a Friday*** is divided into seven key parts. Each part is designed to build on the others. The goal is for you to take just a brief time each day to read and reflect, to put the events and circumstances in your life in perspective, and to receive a mental, emotional, and spiritual lift.

Each of the daily readings was selected to emphasize one of the seven keys. I've added several other features to help you apply and live out the truth that God wants you to know. Therefore, each daily devotional includes:

- **A suggested Scripture reading:** These passages will sometimes relate directly to the key being described, and in other instances the reading will provide necessary background for accurately understanding the truth for that day. Please don't neglect these brief selections from God's Word if you want to gain the full benefit of this book.
- **Key verse(s):** A verse or verses chosen from the Bible reading that expresses a theme of the devotional.
- **A devotional excerpt from *Every Day a Friday*:** A brief story or lesson that I believe will encourage and uplift you.
- **Today's Prayer:** A daily prayer that can serve as a model to help you express your prayer requests, desires, gratitude, and fresh commitments to God. Feel free to adapt these prayers and make them your own. Have a personal conversation with your heavenly Father.
- **Today's Thought:** These are points meant for you to consider thoughtfully after each daily reading. God's Word tells us that our thinking patterns become our acting patterns. The way we talk to ourselves greatly influences our actions. The Today's Thought sections also are meant to encourage you to agree with *what God thinks* of you throughout each day.

These ninety readings should be read at a one-each-day pace so that they carry you through three months or so. My dream is that, day by day, you will grow stronger in your gratitude, your happiness, your faith, and your well-being.

Joel Osteen

DAILY READINGS FROM
EVERY DAY A FRIDAY

PART
I

*Don't Give Away
Your Power*

Happiness Is a Decision

Scripture Reading: Philippians 4

Finally, brothers and sisters, whatever is true, whatever is noble, whatever is right, whatever is pure, whatever is lovely, whatever is admirable—if anything is excellent or praiseworthy—think about such things.

PHILIPPIANS 4:8 NIV

John was ninety-two years old and blind, but he was just as sharp as could be when his wife, Eleanor, went to the Lord. He didn't feel he should live alone, so John decided to move into a nice seniors' home. On the morning of the move, he was up and fully dressed by 8:00 a.m. As always, the elderly gentleman looked impeccable, with his hair perfectly combed and his face neatly clean-shaven.

A cab picked him up and took him to the seniors' home. John arrived early, as was his habit, and waited several minutes before a young aide, Miranda, came to show him to his new room. As John maneuvered his walker through the hallways, Miranda described his room in great detail. She said sunlight came in through a big window, and there was a comfortable couch, and a nice desk area.

Right in the middle of her description, John interrupted her and said, "I love it. I love it. I love it."

Miranda laughed and said, "Sir, we're not there yet. You haven't seen it. Hold on just a minute, and I'll show it to you."

John said, "No, you don't have to show it to me. Whether I like my room or not doesn't depend on how the furniture is arranged. It depends on how my *mind* is arranged. Happiness is something you decide ahead of time."

As wise old John understood, happiness is a choice. When you wake up in the morning, you can choose what kind of day you want to have. You can choose to be in a good mood or you can choose to be in a bad mood.

Today's Prayer

Father, today I choose to be happy. I choose to dwell on things that are good, true, pure, and lovely. Fill me with your peace as I keep my mind on You. In Jesus' Name. Amen.

Today's Thought

Make the most of whatever comes your way, and be looking for God's hand of blessing to carry you into the abundant life He has planned for you!

Every Day Is a Gift from God

Scripture Reading: Ecclesiastes 5

It is a good thing to receive wealth from God and the good health to enjoy it. To enjoy your work and accept your lot in life—this is indeed a gift from God.   ECCLESIASTES 5:19 NLT

According to the authors of the Declaration of Independence, our Creator gave each of us the right to life, liberty, and the pursuit of happiness. Even British prime minister David Cameron recognized this recently when he proposed polling all residents each year to measure their GWB—General Well-Being.

"Well-being can't be measured by money or traded in markets," he said. "It's about the beauty of our surroundings, the quality of our culture, and, above all, the strength of our relationships."

A researcher in Australia found that life goals and choices have as much or more impact on happiness than our body chemistry or genetic makeup. Another study found that half of our happiness is determined by factors other than biology. Ten percent is connected to "life circumstances," and the other 40 percent is dependent on our life decisions.

It's not what happens to you or what you have or don't have that is important; it's how your mind is arranged and the choices you make. When our daughter, Alexandra, was just a little baby and I'd get her out of her crib in the morning, she'd be so excited to hear me coming, she'd start jumping up and down. She'd give me a great big full-body hug with her arm and legs, and then a big kiss.

Why was she so excited? She was just happy for the dawning of a new day. Alexandra was excited to be alive to have another day to enjoy. That's the excitement God has placed inside every one of us. We should never forget how to celebrate each day. But so often as we get older, we let the challenges of life push us down and sadden our spirits.

We have to realize every day is a gift from God. Once this day is gone, we can never retrieve it. If we make the mistake of being negative, discouraged, grumpy, or sour, we've wasted the day. Some people squander year after year, being unhappy because somebody is not treating them right, or because they are not getting their way, or because their plans are not working out as quickly as they would like. I've made up my mind to not waste any more days. I'm celebrating each as a gift from God.

Today's Prayer

Father, thank You for this day that You have made; I choose to rejoice and be glad in it. Help me to see Your hand of blessing at work. Help me to see value in each person I encounter, and help me to see Your love in every situation. In Jesus' Name. Amen.

Today's Thought

Make up your mind to enjoy this day, to have a blessed, prosperous, victorious year. You may have some setbacks and your circumstances may change, but don't let that change your mind. Keep it set on happiness.

Be Glad-Hearted Continually

Scripture Reading: 1 Thessalonians 5

Be happy [in your faith] and rejoice and be glad-hearted continually
[always].   1 Thessalonians 5:16 AMP

I've found that most of the time we have what we need to be happy. We just don't have the right perspective. For instance, you may not be happy with the job you have right now. But if you lost that job and went months without any income, you probably would be very happy to win it back.

You see? You had what you needed to be happy. You just didn't realize it. I know people who are perfectly healthy, but they're never really happy. There's always something bothering them. They want a bigger house or a better job. But if they were to lose their health and then regain it, I'm sure they would be thrilled. They have what they need to be happy.

I hear women complain and complain about their husbands and men complain and complain about their wives: He or she is "just too much of this" or "not enough of that." But if their spouses were suddenly gone and they were lonely month after month, if they didn't have anybody to talk to, if they had nobody to eat dinner with, they might be happy just to get back their "old goats," I mean, their *husbands* or *wives*.

Keep your life in the right perspective. Every one of us has something even right now to be happy about: our health, our jobs, our families, or an opportunity.

I know this couple who constantly complained about their house. It was too small and too far out in the country. It was a source of frustration year after year. But when the economy went down, unfortunately their income went down as well, and they came very close to losing that house. Just before the bank foreclosed on it, they were able to refinance so they could keep their home.

Do you know now they think that house is the greatest thing in the world? They show it off like it's brand-new. What happened? They changed their perspective.

Today's Prayer

Father, You alone are my source of contentment. Thank You for blessing me with everything I need in this life. Fill me with Your joy and satisfaction as I give thanks and praise to You. In Jesus' Name. Amen.

Today's Thought

I've found there are very few things in life that we have to do. "I've got to pay my taxes." No, really, you *get* to pay your taxes. The fact that you have taxes due means that you've made money. That tells me God blessed you with opportunity.

Happiness Is Based on Your Perspective

Scripture Reading: 2 Corinthians 5

We walk by faith, not by sight.

2 CORINTHIANS 5:7 NKJV

I read about these two men who'd been bricklayers for more than thirty years. They were working on a huge skyscraper downtown. One man was always negative, discouraged, constantly complaining, and dreaded going to work. The other man was just the opposite. He was excited to show up each day and had an attitude of faith and enthusiasm about life.

One day a friend came by the job site and asked them separately what they were doing. The first said, "Aw, we're just laying brick. We've been doing this for thirty years. It's so boring. One brick on top of the other."

Then the friend asked the second bricklayer. He just lit up. "Why, we're building a magnificent skyscraper," he said. "This structure is going to stand tall for generations to come. I'm just so excited that I could be a part of it."

Each bricklayer's happiness or lack of it was based on their perspective. You can be laying a brick or you can be building a beautiful skyscraper. The choice is up to you. You can go to work each day and just punch in on the clock and dread being there and do as little as possible. Or you can show up with enthusiasm and give it your best, knowing that you're making the world a better place.

Today's Prayer

Father, today I lift up my eyes to You. Show me Your ways; give me your higher perspective. Help me to take the limits off my life so I can walk with You in joy and victory each and every day. In Jesus' Name. Amen.

Today's Thought

I've found we create much of our own unhappiness. We see what's wrong rather than what's right. We look at what we don't have, rather than what we do have. We don't celebrate each day and appreciate the gift that God has given us.

Count It All Joy

Scripture Reading: James 1

Count it all joy, my brothers, when you meet trials of various kinds.

JAMES 1:2 ESV

How long are we supposed to be glad-hearted? How long are we supposed to have a smile on our faces? As long as people treat us right? As long as we feel okay? As long as the economy is up?

No, the Scripture says, "Be glad-hearted *continually [always]*" (1 Thessalonians 5:16 AMP, emphasis added). That means in the good times and in the tough times, when it's sunny and when it's raining.

When dark clouds are over your head and you feel like life is depressing and gloomy, always remember that right above those dark clouds the sun is shining. You may not be able to see the sun in your life right now, but that doesn't mean it's not up there. It's just blocked by the dark clouds. The good news is, the clouds are temporary. The clouds will not last forever. The sun will shine in your life once again.

In the meantime, keep your joy. Be glad-hearted continually. Don't let a few clouds darken your life. The rain falls on the just and the unjust. That means we all face disappointments, unfair situations, tests, trials, and temptation. But know this: Right past the test is promotion. On the other side of every difficulty is increase. If you go through adversity with a smile on your face and a song in your heart, on the other side there will be a reward.

But so often in the tough times we become discouraged. "I'm down today because business is slow." "I'm upset because I got a bad medical report." Or, "I'm worried about this legal situation."

Human nature tends to turn negative in difficult times. But the Scripture tells us to do just the opposite. James 1:2 tells us we should still be joyful in trying times. That doesn't seem to make sense to some people. "You mean we're supposed to be joyful and glad-hearted in the middle of tough times?" they ask. Yes, that's right, because when you lose your joy, you lose your strength.

You need your strength more than ever in the difficult times, and your strength is dependent on your joy. When you're facing a financial crisis, dealing with an illness, going through a breakup in a relationship, or raising a rebellious child, you need your strength. If you go through those challenges feeling negative, bitter, and discouraged, you will not have the vitality to stand strong and fight the good fight of faith.

You can keep your joy by knowing that on the other side of each test is promotion. On the other side of every setback is opportunity. On the other side of every offense is growth.

Today's Prayer

Father, today no matter what circumstances I face, I choose to count it all joy. I trust that You are with me, You are for me, and You are working behind the scenes to lead me into victory in every area of my life! In Jesus' Name. Amen.

Today's Thought

Just keep reminding yourself, *Even though this is hard, even though I don't understand it, even though it's not fair, I'll keep a good attitude and stay full of joy, knowing that this is not setting me back. It is setting me up for God to bring me through in an even better position.*

Put On the Garment of Praise

Scripture Reading: Psalm 145

Provide for those who grieve...a garment of praise instead of a spirit of despair. They will be called oaks of righteousness, a planting of the LORD for the display of His splendor.   ISAIAH 61:3 NIV

When you put on the garment of praise, that spirit of heaviness has to go. Sometimes you won't feel like doing it. You won't feel like having a good attitude. You won't feel like being grateful. That's why God said to offer up the sacrifice of praise. God knew it would not always be easy. You will have to dig your heels in and say, "God, I don't feel like doing this. It doesn't look like it's ever going to work out. I'm tired, lonely, discouraged. But God, I know You're still on the throne. I know You are good and You are good all the time, so I choose to give You praise. I choose to give You thanks anyway."

When you offer up that sacrifice of praise, supernatural things begin to happen. Scripture tells us the story of the apostle Paul and his companion Silas. They were imprisoned for sharing their faith. They had been unjustly beaten earlier in the day. What were they doing at midnight in their jail cell? Complaining? Having a pity party? Saying, "God, it's not fair. Where were You today?"

No, they were singing praises and giving thanks to God. They were saying, in effect, "God, we know You're bigger than our problems. We know You're still in control. You are able to get us out of here." Sure enough, at midnight there was a great earthquake. The prison doors flew open. The chains fell off, and Paul and Silas walked out as free men.

What started it? They offered up the sacrifice of praise.

Really, anyone can have a good attitude when everything is going well. We can all celebrate and be grateful when we're on the mountaintop, but where are the people who give God praise even as the bottom falls out? Where are the people who rise up each morning and prepare for victory and increase in spite of all the news reports predicting doom and gloom? Where are the people who say, "God, I still praise You even though the medical report wasn't good"?

I believe you are one of those people. I believe you are of great faith. Your roots go down deep. You could be complaining. You could be discouraged. You could have a chip on your shoulder, but instead you just keep giving God praise. You've got that smile on your face. You're doing the right thing even though the wrong thing is happening.

That's why I can tell you with confidence that you are coming into greater victories. Enlarge your vision. Take the limits off God. You have not seen your best days. God has victories in your future that will amaze you. He will show up and show out in unusual ways. You may be in a tough time right now, but remember this: The enemy always fights you the hardest when he knows God has something great in store for you.

Today's Prayer

Father, today I take off heaviness, frustration, and despair and I choose to put on the garment of praise. I thank You that You are here with me now, inhabiting my praises and driving out every enemy. I will bless Your name continually as I stand and see the victory You have in store. In Jesus' Name. Amen.

Today's Thought

You are closest to your victory when it is the darkest. That is the enemy's final stand. Don't be discouraged. Don't start complaining. Just keep offering up that sacrifice of praise.

The Voice of Gladness

Scripture Reading: Matthew 5

*Give praise and thanks to the Lord of hosts, for the Lord is good; for His
mercy and kindness and steadfast love endure forever!*

JEREMIAH 33:11 AMP

The Old Testament prophet Jeremiah wrote, "[There shall be heard
again] the voice of joy and the voice of gladness,... the voices of those
who sing as they bring sacrifices of thanksgiving into the house of the
Lord...[God] will cause the captivity of the land to be reversed and
return to be as it was at first" (Jeremiah 33:11 AMP). I particularly love
two words in that verse; *reversed* and *return*. God is saying when you stay
full of joy, when you learn to offer up the sacrifice of praise, God will turn
things in your favor. He will reverse negative situations. He will return, or
restore, what's been stolen.

But notice that restoration doesn't come from complaining, being negative, or being sour. Restoration takes place when you have the voice of
gladness, the voice of joy. That means you get up in the morning with a
song in your heart. You go out each day with a smile on your face. Things
may not always go your way, but you don't become discouraged. You shake
it off and count it all joy.

When you live that way, you might as well get ready. God will be reversing and restoring. He will reverse finances that have been down. He will

reverse a struggling business. He will reverse a legal situation in your favor. He will reverse a health issue to heal you.

Not only that, God will restore what should have been yours. He will restore the years you lost because somebody did you wrong. He will restore a relationship that's on the rocks. Restoration will occur because you have the voice of joy, the voice of gladness, and you keep offering up that sacrifice of praise.

Learn to count it all joy. Don't be determined never to have problems. Be determined to stay full of joy in the midst of your problems. Arrange your mind in the right direction.

And no matter what comes your way, don't lose your joy. Learn to offer up that sacrifice of praise. If you keep the voice of gladness, the voice of joy, you cannot stay down and defeated.

Today's Prayer

Father, thank You for Your promise of restoration in my life. Thank You for reversing destruction and destroying lack. I receive, by faith, renewed hopes and dreams as I choose to be glad in You always! In Jesus' Name. Amen.

Today's Thought

God has promised He will reverse and restore. Not only that, because you have joy, you will find the strength to outlast every attack, to overcome every obstacle, to defeat every enemy.

Be the Change You Seek

Scripture Reading: John 14

Peace I leave with you; my peace I give you. I do not give to you as the world gives. Do not let your hearts be troubled and do not be afraid.

JOHN 14:27 NIV

Jesus said that we should not let our hearts be troubled or afraid. Notice it's a choice we have to make. He didn't say, "I will make sure your circumstances are perfect. That way you can be happy."

He said, in effect, "The things upsetting you right now don't have to upset you. The people aggravating you, even if they don't change, don't have to aggravate you." If you'll make adjustments and change your approach to life, you can be happy in spite of those circumstances.

I'm asking you today to stop allowing negative people and disappointments and inconveniences to steal your joy. You have to put your foot down and say, "This child gets on my nerves. I love him, but I'm going to rise above it. I won't let this control me." Or, "This grumpy boss jumps down my throat for no reason, but I'm not going to let him ruin any more of my days." That's what it means not to give away your power. You have to be determined to enjoy your life.

A woman once told me about her husband's very obnoxious relative who repeatedly made cutting and demeaning remarks to her. Every time they were at family get-togethers, invariably this man would say something that offended her. She would become upset and it would ruin the whole trip. She reached a point where she didn't want to even go to her husband's family events. Finally, she told her husband, "You've got to do something about that man. He's your relative."

She was expecting the husband to say, "You're right, honey. He shouldn't talk to you like that. I'll go in there and set him straight." But the husband did just the opposite. He said, "Honey, I love you, but I cannot control him. He has every right to his opinion. He can say what he wants to, but you have every right to not be offended."

At first she couldn't understand why her husband wouldn't really stick up for her. Time and time again she would feel upset. If her husband's relative was in one room, she would go to another room. If the man was outside, she would make sure she stayed inside. Her whole focus was avoiding this man. Eventually, she grew weary of allowing him to have such an impact on her life. One day it was like a light turned on. She realized that no one took this man seriously and that she was giving away her power. She was allowing one person who had issues of his own to keep her from becoming the woman she was meant to be.

Today's Prayer

Father, thank You for perfect peace in my heart and mind no matter what is going on around me. Give me wisdom to know what things I can change, and the wisdom to know when You are changing me. In Jesus' Name. Amen.

Today's Thought

So many people today are looking for true, inner peace. They search through relationships, addictions, money, gadgets, and even religion to try to find something that will fill the void inside. But true peace isn't found in anything this world has to offer; it can be found only through a personal relationship with Jesus Christ. Only He can satisfy the longing in our souls and give us true, lasting peace.

Don't Let Anyone Push Your Buttons

Scripture Reading: Proverbs 20

It is an honor for a man to cease from strife and keep aloof from it, but every fool will quarrel. PROVERBS 20:3 AMP

When you allow what someone says or does to upset you, you're allowing that person to control you. When you say, "You make me so mad," what you're really doing is admitting that you're giving away your power. As long as the person knows they can push this button and you'll respond this way, and they can make this remark and you'll get upset, and they know if they go outside, you'll go inside—as long as you keep responding the same way—you are giving them exactly what they want.

People have the right to say what they want, to do what they want, as long as it's legal. And we have the right not to be offended. We have the right to overlook it. But when we become upset and angry, we change. If somebody walks into a room and we grow tense, it's because we're putting too much importance on what that person thinks about us.

What a person says about you does not define who you are. His or her opinion of you does not determine your self-worth. Let that bounce off you like water off a duck's back. This person has every right to an opinion, and you have every right to ignore it.

I've found that some people feel it's their calling in life to point out what others are doing wrong. They're constantly critical, always finding fault. There is nothing they would love more than to keep someone upset, and arguing, and always on the defensive.

Rise above that. You don't need them to agree with you. You don't have to win their approval. Let that go, and just be who God made you to be.

Even the great leader Moses had to deal with relatives who didn't like the woman he'd chosen to marry because she was of a different nationality. They criticized Moses publicly, saying, "We don't agree with this. We refuse to approve of this marriage."

But deep down, Moses knew he was making the right decision. He didn't argue with them. He didn't become upset. He didn't criticize them. He just kept his peace.

You don't have to respond to every critic. You don't have to prove yourself to them. Just stay on the high road and let God fight your battles for you. "The battle is the LORD's... [He] will repay" (1 Samuel 17:47; Romans 12:19 NIV). Some who will cross your path simply don't want peace with you. No matter what you say or do, they will not be won over. Even if you were to change, they would still find some reason to be critical. You have to accept the fact that no matter what you do, some people will never be at peace with you.

When Jesus sent His disciples out into certain homes, He told them to speak peace over each person in each house. And He said, in effect, "If they don't receive it, then the peace you're offering them will come back to you" (see Luke 10:5–6).

That tells me if you do your best to be at peace with people—even if they won't take your peace—the good news is that peace will just come back to you anyway. You'll not only enjoy your peace, but you'll be given their share as well. When you do the right thing when the wrong thing is happening, God sees it and He rewards it.

Today's Prayer

Father, search my heart and mind today. Help me to release offense so I can hold on to peace. Give me wisdom to know when to respond in love and when to hold my tongue so that I can honor You in everything I do. In Jesus' Name. Amen.

Today's Thought

You don't have to have the approval of others in order to be approved by God. Your job is to be the person God made you to be, so overlook offenses and strife so you can live in peace and victory all the days of your life.

Strength Under Control

Scripture Reading: Matthew 5

Blessed are the meek, for they shall inherit the earth.

MATTHEW 5:5 NKJV

Two friends walked into a corner store to buy a newspaper, and the store clerk treated them rudely. One of the friends, after paying, looked directly at the clerk with a grin and said, "I hope you have a great day today."

As they were leaving his friend said, "Is that clerk always that rude?"

"Every single day," the other said.

"Well, are you always that nice?"

"Every single day."

This puzzled his friend, so he asked why.

"I've made up my mind that I'm not going to let one person ruin my day," was the answer.

He had decided not to give control of his mood or attitude to anyone else. That store clerk had every right to be rude and obnoxious, but everyone he mistreated also had the right to keep being happy, kind, and friendly.

When you encounter people who are poisoned inside, don't let it rub off on you. If you sink down to their level and you're cold and rude back to them, you've allowed them to contaminate you. Rise above that. Be a part of the solution, not the problem. You overcome evil with good. If somebody is rude to you, just bless them, smile, and keep moving forward.

Jesus put it this way: "Blessed are the meek, for they will inherit the earth" (Matthew 5:5 NIV). When we hear the word *meek*, many times we think of someone who is weak, shy, and reserved, just a fearful little person. The image is that meek people can't stand up for themselves and everyone runs over them. That's not meek at all. Meekness is not weakness. It's strength under control.

Meekness is like a wild stallion that has been tamed. The horse is still strong, still powerful, and has just as much speed as before he was tamed. The only difference is, now that strength is under control. You can walk up to the horse, pet him, lead him around, probably get on him and ride him. But don't be fooled. He has the same power, the same tenacity; he's just learned how to control it.

When you're a meek person, you don't go around trying to straighten everybody out. You don't respond to every critic. People may be talking about you, but you don't let it bother you.

You may have the power to straighten them out. You may feel like giving them a piece of your mind. Your emotions may tell you, *Get in there. Pay them back. Get even.* Instead, listen to what the apostle Paul told his protégé Timothy: "Be calm and cool and steady" (2 Timothy 4:5 AMP). He was saying, in other words, "Don't give away your power. Keep your strength under control."

Today's Prayer

Father, thank You for the blessing of meekness. I choose today to be a person of self-control. Help me to always be a part of the solution by sowing seeds of peace and love. In Jesus' Name. Amen.

Today's Thought

Keep your strength under control. It's not how proud you are, or how many people you straighten out, or how you can prove yourself. If you argue with a critic and try to prove yourself, all you're doing is sinking to his or her level. Don't fall into that trap. You are an eagle. You can rise above it.

Don't Give Away Your Power

Scripture Reading: 3 John

Beloved, I pray that you may prosper in all things and be in health, just as your soul prospers.   3 JOHN 2 NKJV

Right after the 9/11 terrorist attacks, I was invited to a local television station to be interviewed on a news program. I had to be there early Monday morning around six thirty. I was already tired after our Sunday services and weekend events. The day was cold and raining, and still dark. I didn't really feel like being on television, but I had made the commitment, so I was on my way.

They had told me beforehand to park right up front in this special lot reserved for the people on the program. And so when I arrived, I pulled in there. But when I parked my car, a woman security guard rushed at me like I had just committed a major crime. She was not friendly at all. In fact, she was downright rude.

"Sir, what do you think you are doing?" she said. "You cannot park here. This is reserved for our special guests."

I wanted to say, *Lady, you can't get any more special than me.*

I had to bite my tongue.

"Well, ma'am, I am on the program today, and they told me I could park here," I explained.

"Oh, they don't know what they're talking about," she said. "I run this lot. You have to park outside the gate."

I returned to my car. I couldn't find anywhere to park. I had to go into a little neighborhood far away, and it was still raining. I didn't have an umbrella. And as I ran to the station, with every step I thought, *This is not right. I need to tell somebody about that parking lot lady. I should get her straightened out.*

I was about to give away my power, but instead I walked into the building and forgot all about it.

A couple of hours later, after the show, I walked out and the sun was shining. Do you know the same security guard came up and she was like a different person?

"Oh, Pastor Osteen," she said. "If I had known that was you, I would have let you park there."

I was so glad I bit my tongue. She went on to say, "Do you think you would have time to pray for me?"

I smiled and agreed, though I wanted to say, *I would if I didn't have to walk so far.*

Today's Prayer

Father, thank You for giving me Your peace that passes understanding. Help me to always extend that peace and grace to others. Have Your way in my heart that I may be more like You each day. In Jesus' Name. Amen.

Today's Thought

Make up your mind that you will not accept other people's garbage. They may dump it, but you don't have to receive it. Keep your lid on.

Be Willing to Make a Change

Scripture Reading: Deuteronomy 10

Change your hearts and stop being stubborn. For the LORD *your God is the God of gods and Lord of lords. He is the great God, the mighty and awesome God, who shows no partiality and cannot be bribed.*

DEUTERONOMY 10:16–17 NLT

Sometimes we blame other people or other things for problems that we've created for ourselves. We don't realize that our refusal to change is causing the same problem again and again. I heard about this man who had not been feeling well. He went to see his doctor. The doctor said, "What's wrong?"

He said, "Well, Doctor, lately I've been dizzy and I'm seeing white spots."

The doctor examined him and put him through some tests. Several days later, he called the ailing man back and said, "Sir, I hate to tell you this, but you've got a rare disease and we think you only have about six months to live."

The man quit his job and set off to travel the world and do all the things he'd always hoped to do. He spent more time with his family, and he bought a new sports car. One day he was driving by this famous clothing shop and decided to go in and buy a tailor-made suit and shirt.

The tailor came in and measured his arm length: "Thirty-three inches." Then he measured his waist: "Thirty-two." Next was his pant length: "Thirty-four." And finally the tailor measured his neck and said, "I'm going to make you a size sixteen-and-a-half shirt."

The man said, "No, I wear a fifteen-inch shirt."

The tailor measured his neck again very carefully.

"No, sir," he said. "Look, you wear a sixteen-and-a-half-inch shirt."

The man was very adamant. "No, sir. I wear a fifteen-inch shirt," he told the tailor. "I've worn that size my whole adult life. I want you to make me a fifteen-inch shirt."

The tailor said, "Well, fine. I'll make you a fifteen-inch shirt, but it will be so tight it will make you dizzy and you'll see white spots."

Often, people become set in their ways and refuse to change even when they are hurting. If you are willing to change, if you will make adjustments, many times you will see your "white spots" disappear. You will see your frustrations go away.

Recognize the real source of the problem. If it's you, make a change. If it's someone else, don't let him or her steal your joy. Don't give away your power. Keep your lid on. When somebody tries to dump their garbage on you, just smile, wave at them, and move on. If you'll learn this principle to not give away your power and focus on developing your character, you will enjoy life much more.

Today's Prayer

Father, I come before You with an open and humble heart. Search me and know me. Remove anything that isn't pleasing to You. Show me Your love and lead me the way everlasting. In Jesus' Name. Amen.

Today's Thought

It doesn't matter what happened yesterday, last week, last month, or last year; today is a new day. This moment, you have the power to make a change in your life. Things may be bad all around you. People may be negative, complaining, and discouraged, but don't let that spirit rub off on you. Instead, choose to bless the Lord at all times. Let His praise continually be in your mouth. Remember, the path of the righteous is like the light of dawn shining brighter and brighter until the full day.

Express God's Fullness of Joy

Scripture Reading: Psalm 16

*You will show me the path of life; in Your presence is fullness of joy; at
Your right hand are pleasures forevermore.*   PSALM 16:11 NKJV

Scientists say that humans are programmed to mirror the facial expressions of others they encounter, so your smile is contagious. Make a habit of smiling. Scripture says, "In [God's] presence is fullness of joy" (Psalm 16:11 NKJV).

When you lack joy, you are disconnected from God's presence. When you're sad and frustrated and wear a chip on your shoulder, you've detached yourself from favor, blessing, healing, and promotion. Your happiness supply line has been disconnected.

You have joy deep within you, but sometimes you must push it up higher where we can all see it and share it. Professors at Yale University did a study on how appearance, personality, and attitude influence others. After much in-depth research, they concluded that the single most powerful force of human influence is not looks, height, or personality. Instead, your *smile* is your most powerful tool for influencing others in a positive way.

That explains the saying "If you're not smiling, you're like a person with a million dollars in the bank and no checkbook." Studies have shown that people who smile frequently are promoted more often and end up with higher-paying jobs. Why is that? Don't you prefer being with those who are happy, good-natured, and friendly? Of course, we all do!

I'm known for smiling a lot. My brother, Paul, says I was born with my Happiness Meter set on 98. His was set on 10, but he's working on it. My earliest baby pictures show me smiling. My mother says for the longest time she wondered if I was up to something, but she finally decided it was just my nature.

Years ago, I was in the mall with my wife, Victoria, and she had picked out an outfit to buy. She was still shopping, though, so I offered to take it up to the line at the checkout counter. When I stepped in front of the salesclerk, I smiled and said hello, just being friendly.

The checkout lady smiled back. She was about to ring up the clothes when she stopped and said, "Hang on, I'll be right back." She went into the sales office and came back and said, "This is going on sale this weekend, and I have permission to give you the sale price right now."

I smiled even bigger.

"Thank you so much," I said.

As she was folding the clothes to put them in the bag, she noticed that a little part of the inside lining of one item had come undone.

"This looks like a problem. Do you see that?"

"Oh, yeah, that looks really bad," I said.

"Let me see what I can do," she said.

She headed back to the office and in a few minutes came back.

"Okay, I can cut the price to half the sale price."

I thought, *Man, if I keep smiling, they may owe* me *money!*

Victoria said I should shop with her more often after that. I told her it all started with a smile. If I'd stood at the counter looking like an old grouch, I don't believe the clerk would have gone out of her way to be good to me.

Today's Prayer

Father, I bless You today. Thank You for giving me the fullness of Your joy and strength. Let it overflow in me so that my life can be an expression of Your goodness everywhere I go. In Jesus' Name. Amen.

Today's Thought

When you have God's joy, you have His supernatural strength. There's nothing that can come against you when you are filled with the strength and joy of the Lord. Anytime you feel depleted or overwhelmed by life, just begin to sing a song of praise to Him. Declare His goodness and faithfulness. Draw near to Him, and He will draw near to you. He'll fill you with His joy and strength to live in victory all the days of your life.

Bloom Where You Are Planted

Scripture Reading: Psalm 37

The steps of a good man are ordered by the Lord: *and he delighteth in his way.*   Psalm 37:23 kjv

I was walking through the woods a while back and came to a big open area full of large, tall weeds. For acres and acres, as far as I could see, there were these dead, dried-up, brown, ugly weeds. As I walked through the open field, about a hundred yards in, I saw a beautiful flower. It was so bright, so colorful, so refreshing. It had bloomed right there in the middle of acres and acres of old, ugly, dried-up weeds. And I thought, *Really, that's what God wants us to do. Just bloom where we're planted.*

You may work around a bunch of weeds, but that doesn't have to stop you from blooming. You may be married to an old weed. But the good news is, you can still bloom.

Too many people are negative and discouraged because they don't like where they are. They don't like their spouses. They don't like their jobs. Coworkers are hard to get along with. They don't like where they live. That's not where they want to be.

If negative people have to work late, it sours their day. They are always fighting against something. They are always trying to go somewhere else. But I've learned that God is more interested in changing me than He is in changing my circumstances. As long as I'm sour because I'm not getting my way, discouraged because I'm single and I want to be married, upset because the business isn't growing, that attitude will keep me right where I am.

If you want to see change, if you want to see God open new doors, the key is to bloom right where you're planted. You cannot wait until everything becomes better before you decide to have a good attitude. You have to be the best you can be right where you are.

Put a smile on your face. Be good to people even if they're not good to you. Be grateful for where you live even if it's not where you want to be. When you bloom where you're planted, you're sowing a seed for God to do something new.

The Scripture says, "The steps of a good man are ordered by the LORD" (Psalm 37:23 NKJV). That means as long as we're in faith, where we are is where we're supposed to be.

"That couldn't be right," you say. "I'm uncomfortable. I'm not in a good place. Somebody is not treating me right."

It may be difficult, but God will not allow a challenge to come into our lives unless He has a divine purpose for it. I've found that nothing happens *to* us; it happens *for* us. If we keep the right attitude, God will always use it for our good.

That person who is hard to get along with? He's not happening *to* you, he's happening *for* you. God is using him to grow you up. You're developing character. You're learning to be good to people who are not being good to you. God uses difficult people, like sandpaper, to rub the rough edges off us. The next time you see that person, instead of being upset and all stressed out, just smile real big and say, "Thank you so much for everything you have done for me."

Then you may have to help pick him up off the ground.

Today's Prayer

Father, today I declare that my hope and trust is in You. Even when I don't understand my circumstances I know You are working things out for my good. Help me to bloom where I'm planted so I can live as a testimony of Your faithfulness. In Jesus' Name. Amen.

Today's Thought

If God removed some of the challenges in your life right now, you would not be prepared for what He has in store. When bad times come your way, instead of being negative and complaining, pray for His guidance.

PART
II

Know What to Ignore

If You Complain, You Remain

Scripture Reading: Psalm 66

Make a joyful shout to God, all the earth! Sing out the honor of His name; make His praise glorious. Say to God, "How awesome are Your works! Through the greatness of Your power Your enemies shall submit themselves to You. All the earth will worship You and sing praises to You: They will sing praises to Your name. PSALM 66:1–4 NKJV

It's easy to focus on what's wrong in your life, what you don't have, and how big your obstacles are. But if you are not careful, you will lose sight of all the good things God has done for you. Don't take for granted the family, friends, and opportunities He has blessed you with. If you're in such a hurry and so stressed that you fail to appreciate the gift of today, you'll lose your joy and your ability to be happy every day of the week.

It's all about keeping things in perspective. Business may be slow, but it's the wrong perspective to think, *I'm never going to make it.* The right perspective is to think, *God is supplying all of my needs.*

If you are going through a disappointment, the wrong perspective is, *I should have known this would happen. I never get any good breaks.* The right perspective is to believe that when one door closes, God will open another.

You can put two people in the exact same circumstances and one will be complaining, negative, and just enduring life, while the other will be happy, grateful, and enjoying life. What's the difference? Their perspectives. It's how each chooses to see the situation.

We all have burdens that can steal our joy and cause us to be sour. But if we're to live life happy, we need the foundation of a grateful spirit. I've learned that seeds of discouragement cannot take root in a grateful heart. If you are unhappy today and you've lost your enthusiasm, the quickest way to turn that around is to be more grateful. Instead of looking at what you don't have, thank God for what you do have. Instead of complaining about what's wrong, thank God for what's right.

I've talked to many people who have gone through disappointments. They've lost their jobs, their marriages, or their health. It's difficult for them to see any reason to be grateful. But really, it's a matter of perspective.

I heard of a man who complained he didn't have any good shoes until he met a man who had no feet. His perspective changed then and there.

He thought, *You know what? Maybe I don't have it so bad.*

The truth is, somebody in the world would gladly trade places with you. Somebody would love to be able to breathe like you. Somebody would love to be able to walk like you. Somebody would love to be living where you live. Have you thanked God lately for your family, your friends, your health, and the opportunities He's given you?

If you're complaining about where you are, you won't get where you want to be. If you're complaining about what you have, I believe God will not increase you with more.

Complaining about your old car, your small house, or your spouse won't get you anywhere. Remember this phrase: *If you complain, you remain; but if you'll praise, you'll be raised.*

To keep your life in perspective, try making a list of all the things you are grateful for. Write down ten things that God has blessed you with and put the list on your bathroom mirror. Every morning read over that list two or three times. Do the same every night before you go to bed.

Meditate on the good things God has done. Write down the times God showed up at the midnight hour and made a way where there was no way. Write down the time He protected you from that accident, the time He had you at the right place and you were promoted, the time the medical report said you wouldn't make it but your health suddenly turned around.

Write down the fact that you have healthy children, a roof over your head, and a loving spouse.

Today's Prayer

Father, today I choose to have an attitude of gratitude. I choose to let go of complaining and comparing and instead I choose to focus on my blessings. Help me to keep the right perspective, to always look ahead so I can move forward into the good life You have prepared for me. In Jesus' Name. Amen.

Today's Thought

Meditating on the goodness of God will help you have the right perspective and release your faith, too. When your faith is released, God's power is activated. You will see Him show up and give you something else to put on your list of good things He has done for you.

In Everything Give Thanks

Scripture Reading: 1 Thessalonians 5

In every thing give thanks: for this is the will of God in Christ Jesus concerning you.   1 THESSALONIANS 5:18 KJV

A congregation member told me that his mentally challenged sister couldn't talk or walk or feed herself. She needed constant attention. Growing up, he and other family members helped take care of her. They learned to distinguish among their sister's cries, which were her only way to communicate. There was a hunger cry and a cry for when she wanted to get up and a cry for when she wanted to go to bed, and another cry for when she was thirsty.

The most difficult cry was the sound she made when she had an itch. You see, she couldn't tell them where she felt the itch, so they would go all over her body scratching and scratching, trying to alleviate that itch.

Living with his handicapped sister helped this man appreciate the simple things in life that so many of us take for granted. Scratching an itch is no big deal, until you can't. Then it becomes a very significant matter indeed. It's a big deal that we tell our arms to work and they work. It's a big deal that we open our eyes, and without even thinking about it, we see.

When you get up in the morning and you're tempted to dwell on your problems—how you don't want to go to work and how life's not been fair to you—why don't you turn that around? Instead, thank God that you can scratch your itch. Why don't you thank God that you have no problem breathing? Why don't you look out the window and appreciate the simple things like the sun coming up, the birds singing, and the flowers blooming?

Sometimes we think, *My life is so routine, I just get up and go to work and come home. Nothing exciting is happening. I just do the same thing again and again.* But we should be thankful for routine everyday life. There's nothing ordinary about getting up and going to work. There is nothing ordinary about being able to see, having friends, or having a family. Those are gifts from God.

Too often we don't realize how great we have it until something is taken away. I used to play basketball with a young man named Matt until he started having a problem with his eyes. He had always been very healthy and very active, but his eyes kept bothering him so he went to the doctor. After several tests they told Matt that he had cancer of the eye. The doctor said there was a very good chance he was going to lose his vision.

Matt was so distraught and upset. He went in for an operation, and to the doctor's surprise, they discovered Matt did not have eye cancer. Instead, they found an unusual fungus behind his eye that was affecting his eyesight. They removed it and saved his vision.

When Matt woke up from the operation and heard that his vision was restored, he said, "This is the greatest day of my life."

Think about it. He didn't just win the lottery. He didn't just buy a big new house. He didn't just get a promotion. He simply got the news that his vision was back to normal.

After his eyesight was restored, Matt told me, "Every day I get up in the morning and on purpose I look around. I stare at my children and my wife. I go outside and look at the trees. I bend down and pick up an acorn on the ground."

Because Matt almost lost his vision, being able to see normally has taken on a whole new meaning for him. He will never again take his eyesight for granted. He will be forever grateful for the gift of sight.

Today's Prayer

Father, today and always, I give you thanks and praise. I choose to bless You at all times and in all things. Help me to never take Your gifts for granted and to acknowledge the little miracles around me each and every day. In Jesus' Name. Amen.

Today's Thought

You and I should never take for granted what God has given us. If you can see, if you can hear, if you can walk, if you've got good health, family, friends, and a good job, learn to appreciate each of those gifts.

God Will Make It Up to You

Scripture Reading: 1 Samuel 10

There were some scoundrels who complained, "How can this man save us?" And they scorned him and refused to bring him gifts. But Saul ignored them. 1 SAMUEL 10:27 NLT

Many years ago a young man named Saul was chosen to be the next king of Israel. The prophet Samuel blessed him and called him up in front of the people and said, "He is going to be our next king."

Most of those present were very excited and they congratulated Saul. But when he returned home, many longtime friends ridiculed him.

"Saul is not our king. He's not a leader. He doesn't have what it takes."

They were actually jealous of Saul. They were so insecure, so intimidated, they had to try to push Saul down so they would look bigger.

Remember this phrase: When people belittle you, they are being little themselves. Small-minded people won't celebrate you. Small-minded people will be jealous. They will gossip to make you look bad.

But they are not going where God is taking you. My friend, you are called to be an eagle. You are called to soar, to do great things. But we all have some crows squawking at us, some chickens pecking at us, some hawks attacking us. They are trying to bait us into conflict. Don't get drawn into those battles.

You have an advantage. You're an eagle. You can fly at heights to which no other bird can soar.

Crows love to pester eagles. The eagle is much larger, but the crow is more agile so it can turn and maneuver more quickly. At times the crow will come up behind the eagle and dive-bomb the big bird. But the eagle knows this secret: It can fly at altitudes that the crow cannot fly, as high as twenty thousand feet.

So instead of bothering with the pesky crow and its squawking, the eagle simply rises higher and higher and eventually the crow is left behind.

Do the same when someone is pestering you out of jealousy or spite. Soar above. Leave them behind.

God hears what your critics say, and if you stay in faith, He will make it up to you. Use your energy to improve your skills, to be the best that you can be. And God will bring others across your path who will celebrate and encourage you.

Saul could have easily lost his focus and wasted time defending himself. Many had contempt for the new king, asking, " 'How can this man save us?' And they scorned him and refused to bring him gifts. But Saul ignored them." (1 Samuel 10:27 NLT).

What did he do?

Saul ignored them. One translation says, "Saul paid them no mind" (v. 27 THE MESSAGE).

Follow Saul's wise approach. Pay no mind to jealous people or those who try to bring you down. They don't control your destiny; God does. They are simply distractions. Just stay focused and do what God has called you to do.

Today's Prayer

Father, thank You for empowering me to rise up higher over the adversities of life. I won't look to the left nor to the right. I won't focus on what others say, but only on what You say because Your Word is forever settled in Heaven. I trust that You have my best in mind and You will make up the difference in every area of my life. In Jesus' Name. Amen.

Today's Thought

When you come to the end of your life, you won't have to give an account of it to your critics. Instead, you'll stand before almighty God, the Creator of the universe. You will hold your head high and say, "God, I did my best. I ran my race. I finished my course. I became who You created me to be." That's true fulfillment. That's when you will be rewarded.

Be Your Best, Let God Do the Rest

Scripture Reading: Nehemiah 4

Wherever you hear the sound of the trumpet, join us there. Our God will fight for us! NEHEMIAH 4:20 NIV

I could do no wrong as a boy in my grandmother's eyes. Once, when someone ate her homemade chocolate chip cookies before dinner, I was not even a suspect. Who was it?

"Not my darling Joel," she said. "It may have been one of his sisters, but I know Joel would never do that." My three sisters would be so aggravated. They'd say, "Grandmama thinks Joel is a saint."

I can't help it. I had favor even back then. That's the kind of people God wants to bring you, people who believe the best of you.

Take on this attitude: *I have something great to offer. I am one of a kind. I have a great personality. I have the right looks. And I will not waste time trying to make people love me. I will let that go and trust God to bring me divine connections, people who celebrate me just as I am.*

When Nehemiah was rebuilding the walls of Jerusalem, there were two men at the bottom of the mountain named Tobiah and Sanballat. They were his biggest critics. According to Nehemiah 4, the whole time he was up there working, they were hollering something like this: "Nehemiah, come down here and fight with us. You will never finish that wall. You don't have what it takes."

I love the fact that Nehemiah was focused. They were making a lot of noise, threatening him, calling him names, but he recognized there was no benefit to fighting with them.

When God puts a dream in your heart, there will always be the Sanballats and Tobiahs trying to engage you in battles that don't matter. They may talk mean and say things behind your back. They'll try to lure you into strife. But be disciplined. Recognize when it's a battle that's worth fighting.

A reporter asked Bill Cosby the secret of success. He said, "I don't know the secret of success, but I do know the secret of failure, and that is to try to please everybody." You have to accept that not everybody will support you. Not everybody will like you. Not everybody will understand you. That's okay. Be the best that you can be, and God will take care of your critics.

You don't have time to come down off that wall. You don't have time to convince your critics. You don't have time to argue. You have a destiny to fulfill. You have an assignment to accomplish. Learn to ignore the Sanballats and the Tobiahs. Before long, like Nehemiah, you'll complete your wall and your actions will answer your critics.

Today's Prayer

Father, thank You for causing me to triumph in all things. Today, I choose to stay focused on what You've called me to do. Help me to ignore distractions and battles that don't matter so that I can move forward on the good path You have prepared for me. In Jesus' Name. Amen.

Today's Thought

Stay focused on the main goals God has put in your heart. He will do amazing things. Like David, you will defeat your giants. Like Nehemiah, you will complete your walls. Ignore the distractions, and you will accomplish your goals all the more quickly.

Choose Your Battles Wisely

Scripture Reading: 1 Samuel 17

And David turned away from Eliab . . .

1 SAMUEL 17:30 AMP

As a shepherd boy, David was asked by his father to take meals to his brothers in the battlefield. They had much more prestigious positions as warriors. David was stuck tending the family flock. When he went into the battlefield on his errand, he heard Goliath taunting his people. David asked the men standing around, "What is the prize for the man who defeats this giant?"

"The reward is one of the king's daughters in marriage and no more taxes," they replied.

David saw great value in fighting this battle. There were serious spoils. When David's older brother Eliab heard David talking about fighting the giant, he tried to embarrass him in front of the other men.

"David, what are you even doing out here?" he asked. "And what have you done with those few sheep our father left you with?"

Eliab tried to make David feel small.

I love the way David responded. The Scripture says that David turned and walked away from Eliab. David had feelings just like you and I have. I'm sure he wanted to say, "Oh, Eliab, you think you're something great. You're nothing at all."

He could have chosen to take on his brother. But he didn't take the bait. He focused on what was truly important. Had David wasted his time and energy on his brother, who knows if he would have defeated Goliath?

When you are swept up in petty battles, you risk missing the Goliath put in your path by God to help you fulfill your divine destiny.

Later in his life, King David was walking down the street one day and a young man started making fun of him, calling him names, even throwing rocks. He followed him everywhere, just pestering him, trying to pick a fight, trying to aggravate him.

Finally, King David's friends said, "Do you want us to put a stop to him? Do you want us to shut him up? He is a real pain."

I love the way King David answered. He said, "No, let him keep talking. Maybe God will see that I am being wronged and bless me for it."

That's the attitude you need. It takes all the pressure off. You don't have to retaliate. In fact, your attacker has done you a favor because God will serve as your vindicator. What this person meant for your harm will be used by God to promote you, and blessings will come your way.

Today's Prayer

Father, I humbly come to You today. I release and renounce every negative word spoken over me. I choose to forgive others and hold on to peace. Help me to pick my battles carefully so that I can walk in the victory You have for me. In Jesus' Name. Amen.

Today's Thought

Ask yourself, *Are the battles I'm engaged in worth fighting? Do they have any rewards? Are they furthering me in my journey toward my God-given destiny?*

If it's not between you and your God-given destiny, simply ignore it. Somebody who doesn't want to be your friend or treats you rudely is not worth going to war over.

Silence the Voice of the Accuser

Scripture Reading: Romans 8

There is therefore now no condemnation to them which are in Christ Jesus, who walk not after the flesh, but after the Spirit.

ROMANS 8:1 KJV

Nine-year-old Sam was visiting his grandparents' big farm, where he loved to walk in the woods with his slingshot. He practiced shooting rocks at trees and bottles and cans, but he didn't hit much. You see, Sam was still working on his accuracy.

One evening after a day in the woods, he heard the dinner bell calling him home. As Sam walked toward the house, he spotted his grandmother's pet duck walking by the pond. He never dreamed in a million years he could hit the duck, but just for fun he pulled the slingshot back and let it fly. Believe it or not, the rock hit the duck square in the head. The duck dropped dead without even one last quack!

Sam was shocked. He'd never hit anything he aimed at! He felt terrible.

In a panic, he ran to the dead duck and carried it behind the barn, where he buried it in the woodpile. Sam was headed into the house, feeling terrible still, when he spotted his twelve-year-old sister, Julie, and realized she'd watched the whole sordid affair.

That night after dinner, their grandmother said, "Julie, I'd like you to stay and help me do the dishes if you don't mind."

"Grandmother," she replied, "I'd love to, but Sam said he wants to do the dishes tonight."

As she walked past Sam, she whispered in his ear, "Remember the duck." Trapped, Sam went over and did the dishes.

The next morning their grandfather invited both Sam and Julie to go fishing, but his wife had another plan.

"I really need Julie to stay here and help me do some chores," Grandmother said.

Julie countered, "Grandmother, Sam said he'd like to stay with you and help you out today."

Once again, his sister walked by Sam and muttered, "Remember the duck." Sam did the chores. Julie went fishing.

After a couple of days of hard labor, doing both Julie's chores and his own, Sam had had enough. He fessed up.

"Grandmother, I'm so sorry. I didn't mean to, but I killed your duck."

His kindly grandmother gave him a big hug.

"Sammie, I know what happened," she said. "I was standing at the window watching the whole thing take place. I saw how shocked you were and I've already forgiven you. I've just been waiting to see how long you would let Julie make a slave of you."

Sam's grandmother was not standing alone at that window. God was right beside her. He sees your every mistake. He's not holding anything against you. He's just waiting to see how long you will allow the accuser to make a slave of you.

Romans 8:1 tells us there is no condemnation for those who are in Christ Jesus and who do not walk after the flesh but *according to the Spirit*.

Those last four words are the key. When you make mistakes, if you are in the flesh, you beat yourself up. You feel guilty and unworthy. You live depressed and defeated. Choosing that response will leave you on a dead-end street.

Instead, embrace the Spirit and say, "Yes, I made mistakes. It was my fault. But I know the moment I ask for forgiveness, God will forgive me and forget my mistakes so I can move ahead."

Today's Prayer

Father, thank You for setting me free from all guilt and condemnation. I open the door of my heart to receive Your forgiveness and extend it to others. Thank You for healing me and empowering me to move forward in total victory. In Jesus' Name. Amen.

Today's Thought

God sees your every mistake, every failure, every weakness. The good news is that He has already forgiven you.

Ask God for Mercy

Scripture Reading: Genesis 32

Then the man said, "Let me go, for it is daybreak." But Jacob replied, "I will not let you go unless you bless me." GENESIS 32:26–12 NLT

Mercy says, "God, I believe You will bless me in spite of these mistakes." That's what Jacob did. He had lived his life as a cheater, a deceiver, doing people wrong. He grew tired of living that way. One day he decided he wanted to make things right. He went down to the brook so he could be alone.

Genesis 32 talks about how the angel of the Lord appeared to him in the form of a man. Jacob and the angel began to wrestle. Their struggle went on all night. Jacob said to the angel, "I know who you are, and I'm not letting you go until you bless me."

When the angel saw how determined Jacob was and how he would not give up, he reached over and gave God's blessing to Jacob. Jacob left there a different person. God even changed his name from Jacob to Israel, which means "prince with God."

But can you imagine the nerve of Jacob? Don't you know that took incredible boldness? Here he had practically lived his whole life making poor choices, deceiving, cheating, and lying. He should have felt over-whelmed with guilt, condemnation, all washed up. Somehow he had the confidence not only to ask for forgiveness but also to say, "God, I believe You will bless me in spite of the way I've lived."

Surely God would say, "Jacob, what are you talking about? Are you crazy? You don't deserve to be blessed, not even really forgiven. I'm not going to bless you."

No, God said, in effect, "Jacob, I love the fact that you know who you are: My child, redeemed, forgiven, made worthy. You not only asked to be forgiven, but you also asked for My mercy. And Jacob, if you're bold enough to ask for it, then I'm bold enough to grant it."

That kind of faith grabs God's attention, not when we drag around guilty, condemned, feeling wrong on the inside. No, it's time for us to arise and go to our Father. God is not the one condemning you. That is the accuser. Stop dwelling on those thoughts.

You may have failed, but God's mercy never fails. The sad thing is, most people accept the condemnation quicker than they accept God's mercy. Don't let that be you. Shake off the guilt. Shake off the negative mistakes from the past. Don't go another minute in regret, feeling bad about yourself.

The moment you asked for forgiveness, God forgave you. Now you do your part and unload the baggage. Leave the guilt right where you are. Don't take it with you. Leave the bag of regrets. Leave the bag of failures. Leave the bag of condemnation right where you are.

Today's Prayer

Father, today I come boldly before Your throne of Grace asking for mercy. Your Word says that You are no respecter of persons and if You did it for Jacob, You'll do it for me. I receive forgiveness, I receive Your love, and I receive every blessing You have in store for me. In Jesus' Name. Amen.

Today's Thought

If you learn to silence the voice of the accuser, guilt and condemnation cannot weigh you down. You will live a life of freedom, rising higher, overcoming obstacles, and accomplishing dreams.

You Are Made in God's Image

Scripture Reading: Acts 10

God does not show favoritism but accepts from every nation the one who fears him and does what is right.　　　Acts 10:34–35 niv

My mother had polio as a child. She wore braces on her legs. Today, one of her legs is much smaller than the other. When she buys shoes, she has to pick up two pairs because her feet are two different sizes. But one thing I've always loved about my mother is that she never allows her "differences" to stop her from pressing forward.

She could have shrunk back and tried to hide her differences and felt insecure, but instead she has a "no-excuses" mentality. She knows she's been made in the image of almighty God. She wore shorts and dresses growing up, never trying to hide her legs. She still wears dresses today.

My mother is seventy-seven years old and still showing off her legs! Don't let her fool you. She loves it!

The effects of her polio never stopped her from working in the yard and around the house or wanting to help others. She could have thought, *I can't pray for others to heal. My legs are not well,* but she did not allow her own health issues to stop her from praying for others in need of healing.

You don't have to be perfect for God to use you. Take the hand you've been dealt and make the very most of it. Believe that God can turn situations around. Believe that He'll bring healing. Even if it doesn't happen, you can still honor God by being the best you can be right where you are.

My sister Lisa was born with symptoms similar to cerebral palsy. The doctors told my parents that she'd never be able to walk, never be able to feed herself. They said, "You might as well prepare to take care of a disabled child." Of course, my parents were devastated. They prayed. They believed. They stood in faith, and little by little Lisa got better and better. Today she is perfectly normal. She's on staff with us here, and she often ministers for us.

Today's Prayer

Father, thank You for loving me and making me in Your image. Help me to see myself as the masterpiece You created and to use my gifts and talents to bring You glory in everything that I do. In Jesus' Name. Amen.

Today's Thought

Where the Spirit of the Lord is, there is freedom—and God's freedom is free for everyone! God wants to pour out His abundant blessing on all who honor Him and do what is right. That means God does not judge you based on physical conditions. He looks at your heart. He looks at the gifts He's placed inside you. Focus on honoring Him and doing what is right, and you'll see His hand of blessing in every area of your life.

DAY 9

Live a No-Excuses Life

Scripture Reading: Jeremiah 20

If I say I'll never mention the LORD or speak in his name, his word burns in my heart like a fire. It's like a fire in my bones! I am worn out trying to hold it in! I can't do it!　　　　JEREMIAH 20:9 NLT

If you feel you are disadvantaged or disabled, instead of saying, "It's not fair, God," your attitude should be: *God, I'm ready. I know You have something great in store for me. I refuse to live defeated and depressed. I know this disadvantage is simply another opportunity for You to show up and show out.*

That's exactly what Tony Melendez did. He was born without any arms. As a little boy he had a desire to play the guitar. Something inside said, *You're supposed to sing and write music.* Tony didn't know any better. He could have said, "Too bad for me. I'd love to play the guitar, but I don't have any arms." Instead, his attitude was, *I may not have any arms, but I do have feet. I may not have any fingers, but I do have ten toes.*

Tony learned to play the guitar with his feet. He can play better with his feet than most of us can play with our hands.

When God puts a dream in your heart, when He puts a promise on the inside, He deposits in you everything you need to accomplish that dream. God wouldn't have given Tony the desire without giving him the ability. It just wasn't the "normal" way. Tony had to be bold enough to say, "I am living a no-excuses life. Yes, this may look like a handicap. Yes, in the natural, I may have a disadvantage, but I know with God there are no handicaps. I know when God made me, He wasn't having a bad day. He made me with a purpose, with a destiny to fulfill, and I will do my best to bring honor to Him."

Tony has a "can-do" attitude. Other people are hung up on what they can't do or what they don't have, but those "disadvantages" are really advantages just waiting to come to life.

Today, Tony has unprecedented favor. He has traveled to more than forty countries, singing and sharing his story of faith. God is using him to do great things.

Most people never have to deal with anything as challenging as Tony's missing limbs. Yet people often allow more common problems such as divorce, job loss, or financial challenges to overwhelm them. They need to adopt Tony's no-excuses mentality, press forward, and give God time to turn their liabilities into assets.

Today's Prayer

Father, You said in Your Word that I am fearfully and wonderfully made. Help me to look past what I see in me as disadvantages. Help me to live a "no-excuses" life and to use what You have given me to glorify You and be a blessing to others. In Jesus' Name. Amen.

Today's Thought

God will never ask you to do something without putting His anointing and ability inside you. In the Scripture, God put a promise in Jeremiah that he would be a prophet and speak to the nations. Jeremiah felt afraid, had obstacles, and battled his own fears and apprehensions, but inside, he had a promise.

God Will Turn Your Disadvantages to Advantages

Scripture Reading: Luke 19

Jesus said to him, "Today salvation has come to this house, because this man, too, is a son of Abraham. For the Son of Man came to seek and to save the lost." LUKE 19:9–10 NIV

Luke 19:1–10 tells the story of a man named Zacchaeus. He had a disadvantage. He was short. No doubt, when he was growing up, the other children teased him, calling him "Shorty" or "Peanut." I can imagine he wanted to be more like everyone else. But understand, God makes us the way we are on purpose.

One day, Zacchaeus heard that Jesus was coming through his town. All the people were lined up on the streets trying to get a glimpse of Him. Zacchaeus didn't have a chance. He was standing at the back and could not see over anyone. He could have easily given up and felt sorry for himself. Instead, he climbed a tree and had a great view, maybe the best. His disadvantage turned into an advantage.

When Jesus came down the street, He looked above the crowd and saw Zacchaeus in the tree. Jesus called out to Zacchaeus and asked to have dinner at his house.

If Zacchaeus had been a "normal" height, he wouldn't have climbed the tree and caught the attention of Jesus in the crowd. But because of his "handicap," Zacchaeus climbed higher and reaped one of the highest possible rewards!

Take a higher perspective as Zacchaeus did. Look at your supposed liability and consider that it may be an advantage. I realize now my laid-back, easygoing, soft-spoken personality is an asset. For me to act like someone else would not work. I've accepted who I am and so has our congregation.

Today's Prayer

Father, thank You for uniquely designing everything about me. Thank You for creating me on purpose and for a purpose. Today I dedicate every area of my life to You knowing that You will take those things that seem to be disadvantages and turn them around for my good. In Jesus' Name. Amen.

Today's Thought

We all have characteristics that can feel like disadvantages, things that seem to make life harder on us. But what you think is a disadvantage, God will turn around to be an advantage so you can move forward into the abundant life He has for you.

You Can Have the Last Laugh

Scripture Reading: Romans 12

Dear friends, never take revenge. Leave that to the righteous anger of God. For the Scriptures say, "I will take revenge; I will pay them back," says the LORD.

ROMANS 12:19 NLT

Many years ago my father, John Osteen, received a letter from another minister that was very mean, critical, and hurtful. He accused my father of things that were totally false. My father was extremely hurt and a little angry. He wrote his attacker the meanest, ugliest letter he could come up with. He ripped his critic apart.

Then, he sealed the scathing letter in an envelope, walked to the end of the driveway, and put it in the mailbox for pickup.

As my father walked back to the house, an inner voice said, *You got even, didn't you?*

"Yeah, I got even," Daddy replied.

You feel better, don't you?

"Yeah, I feel better."

You paid him back, didn't you?

"Yeah, I paid him back."

Then the voice said, *You sure did. You paid him back evil for evil.*

My father gulped. He could feel that conviction. He knew God was speaking to him. He realized he had responded in the wrong way.

Daddy returned to the mailbox, retrieved the letter, and tore it up. He never sent it; never said another word about it to the man. He chose to let God be his avenger. He chose to let God make his wrongs right.

Sixteen years later my father received a phone call from the man who had attacked him. He was weeping. He said, "Pastor Osteen, that letter I sent you was so wrong. I feel so bad. Can you forgive me?"

God knows how to bring justice in your life. It may not happen overnight, but it will happen.

We all go through situations in which we are treated unfairly. Maybe somebody is gossiping about you, or picking on you, trying to make you look bad at school or work. The natural response is to defend yourself or to strike back. Human nature wants to get revenge. We like to get even. But the Lord says, "Vengeance is Mine" (Deuteronomy 32:35 NKJV). That means God will make your wrongs right. God wants to repay you for every unfairness. He is a God of justice.

The bottom line is this: God wants you to have the last laugh.

If you take matters into your own hands, God will step back and say, "You go ahead. You don't need My help." But if you learn to stay on the high road, control your emotions, and let God be your avenger, He will show up and say, "All right. Let Me go to work."

Today's Prayer

Father, thank You for being my Vindicator. Right now I release my desire to get even with those who have hurt me. I release any offense, anger, or bitterness and I choose forgiveness. Fill me with Your peace as I surrender all things into Your loving and capable hands. In Jesus' Name. Amen.

Today's Thought

You can either avenge yourself or let God be your avenger, but you can't have it both ways. If you take matters into your own hands, then God is going to step back and say, "Go ahead, do it your way. Looks like you don't need My help." But if you choose to stay on the high road and say, "No, I'm going to let God be my avenger and trust God to bring justice into my life," you are leaving the way open for God to move mightily on your behalf.

God Knows How to Avenge You

Scripture Reading: Proverbs 16

*When the LORD takes pleasure in anyone's way, he causes their enemies
to make peace with them.*   PROVERBS 16:7 NIV

Don't take matters into your own hands. If you'll let God be your
vindicator, He will bring justice and He will promote you right in front of
those trying to make you look bad.

I met a man in our church lobby who said, "I was your biggest critic.
I was always talking about you, blogging against you. And I came to one
of your services to find something else to criticize. But I liked it so much
I came back the next week. That was six months ago. I haven't missed a
service yet. Now I'm your biggest supporter." He reached out and shook
my hand.

God will cause your enemies to shake your hand, too. You may have
people you're at odds with. You may have a coworker or a family member
who holds a grudge against you. Maybe you've done your best to be kind
and respectful and acted toward them just the opposite of what they've
shown you. Maybe the kinder you are, the more hateful they are.

It would be easy for you to be bitter toward them, but don't sink to their
level. Keep doing the right thing. God is a God of justice. He knows how
to change people's hearts. It may take a week. It may take a year or twenty-

five years. But God promises that one day those who would hurt you now will reach out and shake your hand.

Today's Prayer

Father, I humbly come before You giving You all that I am. Thank You for filling me with Your love. Thank You for causing my enemies to be at peace with me as I live a life that is pleasing to You. In Jesus' Name. Amen.

Today's Thought

God wants you to live in peace. He doesn't want to see you worried and frustrated, striving to fight your battles with your own strength. He wants to fight your battles for you. He wants to be the hero of your story.

God Will Multiply You Exceedingly

Scripture Reading: Genesis 17

I will make My covenant [solemn pledge] between Me and you and will multiply you exceedingly. GENESIS 17:2 AMP

A friend of mine, Larry, is in the real estate business. He is a hard worker who has always given his job one hundred percent and maintained a great attitude. However, the owner of the firm where he started out, Charles, treated him poorly. He refused to listen to any of my friend's suggestions and made things difficult. Larry continued to do his best, but inevitably the owner fired him.

To his credit, Larry didn't become bitter. Instead, he started his own real estate company and became extremely successful. He forgot all about Charles, but God is a God of justice. He never forgets what you are owed. You may let it go, but God doesn't let it go. He makes sure you get everything you deserve.

Several years later, Charles had to downsize his business. He needed a new building, and the one he found was owned by Larry. The former boss nearly passed out when he walked in and realized that he was about to rent a building owned by the man he had fired.

You can believe that this time, Charles listened carefully to everything Larry had to say. He treated his former employee with respect and honor. He valued his opinion. Today, Charles pays rent—a very steep rent—to

Larry. That's God causing your enemies to shake your hand. That's God giving you the last laugh.

God wants to promote you in front of your opponents. Part of His justice is vindicating you so those who said you would fail see you succeeding and accomplishing your dreams.

A minister I know spent more than fifty years traveling the world and doing good. He was beloved everywhere he went. But the newspaper in his hometown was always finding something wrong with his church. He could do a hundred things right. They wouldn't report on that. They would find the one thing he did wrong and make a big deal about it. This went on year after year.

My minister friend had an interesting perspective. He said, "If it had not been for that newspaper, I would not have accomplished so much. They not only kept me on my knees, they also gave me fuel to prove them wrong. Their critical spirit, that injustice, put me in a position to receive God's favor in a greater way."

He went on to build a big university in that town. Thousands of young people have attended. It seemed the least likely place for him to be blessed, the least likely place for him to accomplish his dreams. But God says, "That's where I prepare the table. That's where I want to increase you. That's where I want to show you unusual favor."

Today's Prayer

Father, thank You for Your faithfulness in my life. Thank You for preparing a table before me in the presence of my enemies. By faith, I receive Your promise to bless and multiply me as You lead me into victory all the days of my life! In Jesus' Name. Amen.

Today's Thought

God is in the multiplication business. It doesn't matter what your need is today, God wants to increase you. God can make you seem bigger than you really are. He can make you look more powerful. He knows how to multiply your influence, your strength, and your talent.

God Will Bless You Where You Are

Scripture Reading: Romans 4

Against all hope, Abraham in hope believed and so became the father of many nations, just as it had been said to him.   ROMANS 4:18 NIV

According to Genesis 26:1, there was once a great famine in the land of Israel. For many months there was a drought that turned the region into a wasteland. A young man named Isaac was about to pack up and move to another place. But God said, "No, Isaac. I don't want you to leave there. I'm going to bless you right where you are."

Isaac obeyed God's command and planted his fields. The Philistines who lived there didn't like Isaac and were already jealous of him. This added fuel to their fire and their ridicule of him. But Isaac, whose name means "laughter," just stayed in peace.

Several months later all those who had mocked and criticized Isaac were amazed to see his fields. They couldn't believe it.

The Scripture says that Isaac "the same year reaped a hundredfold" (Genesis 26:12 NIV) more than he planted, right there in the midst of the famine.

Isaac's critics were dumbfounded, but he knew God had set the table and blessed him.

At some point, you may be tempted to run from a bad situation, but I want you to have a new perspective. You do not have to leave in order to be blessed. God wants to bless you right where you are.

Part of His vindication is promoting you so the opposition can see it. Your attitude should be: *They may be laughing now, but I know this challenge is preparing the way for God to promote me. They meant it to hold me down, but God is going to use it to thrust me forward!*

You may be dealing with critics, naysayers, backbiters, backstabbers, those who are jealous and who say you'll never make it. Let me assure you that God will give them a clear view of your table. He'll make sure they see you promoted, honored, and accomplished.

Let God be your avenger. Let God right your wrongs. If you let Him do the avenging, you will always come out better. He will even cause your enemies to end up shaking your hand. They may be laughing now, but know this: God is faithful. In the end, you will have the last laugh. He will bring justice into your life.

Today's Prayer

Father, thank You for your promise to bless me right where I am. I believe that You will multiply me even in the midst of famine. Though thousands fall all around me, You will preserve me. I receive Your peace and rest today knowing that You are directing my every step as I submit my ways to You. In Jesus' Name. Amen.

Today's Thought

Don't focus on the impossible circumstances, focus on the God who makes the impossible possible! Keep looking through your eyes of faith, because He has blessing and victory in store for you.

PART
III

Live Without Crutches

The Gift of Good-Bye

Scripture Reading: Proverbs 22

Do you see someone skilled in their work? They will serve before kings.
PROVERBS 22:29 NIV

I was nineteen years old when I returned from college to begin Lakewood's television outreach. My television production experience was limited, so we hired an experienced producer from California. He was in his sixties and had produced major-league sports and network morning shows in a long career.

He was knowledgeable, talented, and had a great personality. He was fun to be around. We hit it off from the very start. I would come in early, stay late, go to dinner with him, and hang out. I watched very carefully how he put the programs together and how he chose certain camera shots.

I was learning so much from him. I used to think, *I could never do what he does. He is so creative. He can write. He can direct. I'm just not that talented.*

The veteran producer had been mentoring me for about a year when he came in one day and announced that he was leaving in a month.

"No way," I said. "You cannot leave me with this job. I don't know what to do."

He assured me that I'd do just fine.

"You've watched me for a year, and I've watched you, too," he said. "You can handle the job by yourself now."

I wasn't convinced. I pleaded with him to stay, offered him a raise and more time off, but he insisted that it was time to move on.

The first couple of weeks after his departure, I was so nervous. I didn't know what I was doing. I called him every other hour with questions. But in a month I started to feel more comfortable. In six months I thought, *I'm pretty good at this*. A year later I said, "What did I ever need *him* for?"

I realize now that my mentor did me a favor by leaving. He forced me to stretch and to use my God-given talents. If he had not departed, I never would have stepped into my divine destiny.

Likewise, in your life, your destiny is not tied to your mentor's. His or her leaving will launch you ahead. It's not a step back, it's a step up. When someone walks away, it's not an accident. God will open new doors. You will discover greater strength and new talents. God may be preparing to bring in someone even *better* for the future.

Today's Prayer

Father, thank You for the people You have placed in my life to sharpen me as iron sharpens iron. Thank You for increasing my ability, my talents, and my influence. Help me to discern the times and seasons and help me to be willing to let go of the old so I can embrace the new opportunities You have prepared for me. In Jesus' Name. Amen.

Today's Thought

Don't get trapped into thinking that "good enough" is good enough. You are created for more than just average. Today is a new day, and there are new heights for you to climb. Pursue what you love and keep developing that area of your life. Take a class or find a mentor who will help you take full advantage of your skills. As you do, you'll rise higher and higher. You will stand before leaders and rulers, and you'll live the blessed life God has in store for you.

Let Go to Move Ahead

Scripture Reading: Proverbs 20

It is an honor for a man to cease from strife.

PROVERBS 20:3 AMP

A crutch is a temporary tool we use for walking following an injury to a leg or foot. Once the injury is healed, we put the crutch away and walk on our own. The word *crutch* is also used to describe something or someone we may rely on short-term to help us get through a period of challenge. The term takes on a bad connotation, though, when used to describe something that we've become unnecessarily dependent upon, usually to the detriment of our physical, mental, or emotional progress.

A crutch is supposed to be temporary, just until we heal, or until we can get by on our own. It's not supposed to be permanent, even when our crutch is someone important to us. One of the hardest things to accept is that not everyone is meant to be in our lives forever. Some people are meant to be with you for the long term, of course—your spouse, your children, your siblings, your parents, and your closest friends. But then there are those God brings across your path for a season, maybe a mentor, a teacher, or a guide of some sort to help you through a certain stage of life or a difficult time.

If God didn't move them away, we would become too dependent. Instead of helping us, they would hinder us. Their presence might limit our growth.

You have to be big enough to recognize when someone's part in your life story is over. It doesn't mean the person is bad. You can still be friends. You can still love and respect each other. But you must accept that everything changes. To move forward, you have to let go.

Just as God supernaturally brings people into our lives, He will supernaturally move some out. When a person walks away and you think you can't live without them, that's God saying, "It's time for you to go to a new level."

You don't need someone to constantly think for you, drive you, believe in you, and encourage you. You can do that for yourself. If you are to keep growing, eliminate your dependency on crutches.

Don't try to talk people into loving you. Don't try to persuade them to stay beyond their usefulness. *Let them go.*

I saw this principle in action during my father's ministry whenever someone announced he or she was leaving the congregation. They expected my father to be down and discouraged that they were leaving. So the person was often shocked when he seemed happy at their departure.

He never tried to talk them into staying, or to convince them they were making a mistake. My father was always very gracious. He always thanked them, prayed over them, and then he walked them to the door. He didn't say it, but I know what he was thinking: *The sooner you go, the better for both of us.*

You want people in your life who are supposed to be there. When God wants them present in your life, they don't find fault in everything you do, and you don't have to manipulate them to stay. That's what I love about our church members at Lakewood. There are so many, I can't know most of them by name. I can't call them personally. But I know they don't come to church because they need me. They come because God led them to our church. They don't need me to touch them. They need God to touch them.

Today's Prayer

Father, today I submit every relationship in my life to You. I trust that you are connecting me to the right people, and removing people who are no longer tied to my purpose. Give me wisdom and grace to navigate change and rise up higher in the gifts and talents You have given me. In Jesus' Name. Amen.

Today's Thought

When God sends people your way, you don't have to play up to them and do everything perfectly to keep them happy. You don't have to walk on eggshells trying not to offend them. You don't need friends who are hard to please. If someone tries to manipulate you like that, let go and walk away. You don't need anyone else to fulfill your destiny.

You Have a Direct Connection to God

Scripture Reading: Romans 1

The Angel of the LORD appeared to him, and said to him, "The LORD is with you, you mighty man of valor!" JUDGES 6:12 NKJV

A congregation member once said to my father, "My friend prayed for me. He said God wants me to go to Africa and be a missionary. What do you think?"

My father said, "It's your decision, but if you go to Africa based on his advice, make sure you take that friend so he can tell you when to come back home!"

You don't need someone else to tell you what God wants *you* to do! Walk with God on your own. I was reminded of this when a young lady asked my advice on a relationship issue.

"This man that I hardly even know is saying God told him that I was supposed to marry him."

I had to laugh because she is a beautiful young lady. Then I told her not to take this guy too seriously, because every single guy who sees her will think the same thing. "He's just the only one bold enough to tell you," I said.

You can hear from God for yourself. You don't need a crutch. Listen to the *still, small voice* inside you. God sometimes speaks to us through an impression that is always consistent with His written Word, the Bible.

Judges 6–7 tells the story of a man named Gideon who faced three armies marching against him and his men. As Gideon prepared for the battle, God said, "You have too many people with you. If you win with this many, you'll be tempted to think you did it on your own strength and I won't get the credit I deserve."

To trim the numbers, God told him to let everybody who was afraid go home.

I can imagine Gideon was depressed and fearful he'd lose the battle because he didn't have enough warriors.

But God wasn't done trimming down his army.

"Gideon, you still have too many people," God said.

His army dropped from 32,000 to just 300 by the time God was done.

I'm sure Gideon thought his depleted forces would be wiped out.

But it's not important how many you have on your side. What is important is having the right people on your side. Gideon and his 300 men defeated tens of thousands of enemy troops.

Today's Prayer

Father, thank You for giving me a direct connection to You through the power of Jesus Christ. I believe that You are speaking to me, I believe that you are teaching me to hear Your voice. Thank You for Your peace and joy as I seek You with my whole heart. In Jesus' Name. Amen.

Today's Thought

You may feel underqualified sometimes. You may feel that you can't do it alone. But as long as you walk in faith, you are never alone. What you lack, God will provide.

Follow What God Has Put in Your Heart

Scripture Reading: Galatians 1

Am I now trying to win the approval of human beings, or of God? Or am I trying to please people? If I were still trying to please people, I would not be a servant of Christ. GALATIANS 1:10 NIV

When I announced plans to move our church to the former Compaq Center, 99 percent of the congregation supported the move. Most were very excited. But there was one very vocal opponent. He made sure I heard about his opposition. Every week after the service, he would come find me in the visitors' reception area. He would say, "You know, your father said he would never move the church. You're making a big mistake. And I just want to let you know if you move it, I'm not going to come."

I thought, *Is that a promise?*

Everyone has a right to an opinion. But he didn't know what I was feeling on the inside. He didn't know what God was speaking to me. I could not allow him to stop the move. The easy thing is to play it safe. But be strong and follow what God has put in your heart.

I've learned I may have to displease a few people so I don't displease God. I never like to see anyone leave the church, but if I'll stay true to my heart, I believe for every one person who leaves the church, God will send me two dozen more in return.

Too many people get their worth and value out of what other people think. Because of insecurity they are constantly playing up to people, trying to win favor, trying to meet every expectation. When you do that, you can end up being controlled and manipulated. This allows people to put you in a box and make you into something you are not. There are people who are not following their dreams because they are so concerned about falling from the good graces of others.

If others' approval is based on your meeting all their demands and keeping them happy, they are not true friends; they are manipulators. There is a real freedom when you realize that you don't need other people's approval because you have almighty God's approval.

Don't spend your life trying to keep everyone around you happy. Some people don't even want to be happy. You have to be secure enough to say, "I love you, but I won't allow you to control me. You may not give me your blessing, but that's okay. I have God's blessing." Tell yourself that you are not going to be a people pleaser; you are going to be a God pleaser.

Today's Prayer

Father, thank You for leading and guiding me with Your peace and joy. Help me to focus on pleasing You and You alone so that I can run my race, fulfill my destiny, and live the life You have in store for me. In Jesus' Name. Amen.

Today's Thought

If you let other people control you and you feel that you have to meet all their demands, the day you finally wise up and get tired of being manipulated, they will just cut you off. It is much better to trust God to give you direction for your life.

God Will Reward You for Seeking His Kingdom

Scripture Reading: Luke 18

Everyone who has given up house or wife or brothers or parents or children, for the sake of the Kingdom of God, will be repaid many times over in this life.   LUKE 18:29–30 NLT

When my mother, Dodie, was twenty-six years old, my father decided to leave the church that he had been pastoring for many years. The old congregation wasn't really behind his new doctrine of faith and healing and miracles. My mother had longtime friends in that church. Instead of celebrating my mother's new beginning, those friends wouldn't have anything to do with her.

Lifelong friends walked away, all because my father decided to strike out on his own. I love what Jesus said in Luke 18:29–30: "Everyone who has given up house or wife or brothers or parents or children, for the sake of the Kingdom of God, will be repaid many times over in this life" (NLT). Notice it doesn't say when you get to heaven, God will bless you. It says, right here on the earth, if you give up anything for God's sake, He will reward you more than you can even imagine.

My mother lost all of her friends. They wouldn't give her their approval anymore. But can I tell you that God is a faithful God? My mom found many more new friends, even more than she could ever have imagined.

God will always finish what He started. No matter how dark it looks, no matter how long it's been, no matter how many people are trying to push you down; if you will stay in faith, God will complete what He started.

Today's Prayer

Father, today I seek first Your kingdom. I trust that You are leading me into blessing and victory. I release those who do not support what You've placed in my heart. I forgive them and love them. Thank You for rewarding me as I diligently seek after You. In Jesus' Name. Amen.

Today's Thought

At some point God will ask you to prove your faith. It wouldn't be as difficult if all of your friends and family members encouraged you to do it, too. But most of the time, your friends will advise you to stay put. You should listen to the Father in heaven, who will reward you. Keep standing, keep believing, because soon you will rise up into the higher places He has in store for you.

God Will Not Forsake You

Scripture Reading: Jeremiah 1

Before I formed you in the womb I knew and approved of you.

JEREMIAH 1:5 AMP

When Jesus told Peter that He was going to Jerusalem "[to] suffer many things," Peter said, "Far be it from You, Lord; this shall not happen to You!" (Matthew 16:21–22 NKJV).

Peter loved Jesus. He was concerned about Him, but he didn't understand Jesus' destiny. Others may not understand what God has put in your heart. You don't have to write them off, but you do have to be strong and follow your destiny, with or without their approval.

That's what Jesus did. He looked at Peter and said, "Get behind Me, Satan! You are an offense to Me, for you are not mindful of the things of God, but the things of men" (v. 23 NKJV). He was strong. He was firm. But He wasn't disrespectful.

He didn't say, "I'm never going to speak to you because you don't agree with Me." Jesus simply spoke the truth in love and went on to fulfill His destiny without Peter's approval.

In the same way, you will not become everything God has created you to be if you must have the approval of everyone around you. I would love to tell you that all of your family and friends will be there to cheer you on and encourage you and support you. Most of the time, though, somebody will be jealous. Someone won't understand. Some will try to belittle or discredit you.

You can't please everyone, so let those who disapprove know you love them and that the only approval you need is God's. Tell them, "I have almighty God's approval, and He has promised if I give up anything for His sake, He will reward me greatly."

That's a powerful attitude. When you are secure enough in who you are, you will be confident in the destiny in front of you. Keep being your best. Do that, and nothing will stop you.

The Creator of the universe will break down every barrier and take you to where you're supposed to be. Keep a good attitude. Shake off the negative voices. Don't pay any attention to the naysayers trying to discredit you and make you look bad. If you stay in faith, the more they talk negatively of you, the higher God will take you.

Today's Prayer

Father, thank You for approving and loving me. Because I am approved by You, I don't have to live for the approval of people. Help me to always walk in Your Truth as I press forward into the destiny You have prepared for me. In Jesus' Name. Amen.

Today's Thought

Don't be held back by the fear of people abandoning you. If they leave you, you don't need them. God said He would never leave us or forsake us. We know God can't lie. So know that if someone withholds approval, it's no big deal because you have God's approval.

Focus on Winning the Favor of God

Scripture Reading: Psalm 75

Promotion cometh neither from the east, nor from the west, nor from the south. But God is the judge: he putteth down one, and setteth up another.

PSALM 75:6–7 KJV

Our friend Joyce Meyer is a great Bible teacher. She started her ministry in a small classroom in a little church. Every week about forty people would attend her Bible study.

Her husband, Dave, would sit in the front row supporting her. One week after class the pastor called them aside and said, "Dave, this is out of order. You should be up there teaching, and Joyce should be sitting on the front row supporting you."

They were young and didn't want to disappoint the pastor because he could put them out of that church where all of their friends went. This pastor was a good man, but he didn't know what God had put in Joyce's heart. He didn't know she had an incredible gift to teach.

Out of respect for the pastor, Dave began teaching and Joyce took a seat in the front row. Now, it was good that they were willing to come under authority. I'm not saying that we should be rebellious and not ever take advice. But I am saying that we shouldn't let other people run our lives. Some people can't even run their own lives, after all.

Several weeks went by and Joyce was miserable. Dave was miserable, too. He didn't like teaching. That's not what he was called to do. One day

Joyce finally began teaching again. Sure enough, the pastor asked them to leave. He no longer approved or accepted them.

Thank God that Joyce knew she had God's approval! She's done well ever since.

When you come to the end of your life, you won't stand before other people. You will stand before God. It's not a good excuse to say you didn't fulfill your destiny because you had to please your friends or coworkers instead.

Run your race. Fulfill your destiny. Know that it's great to have the approval of others, but it's better to please God.

Save your time and energy for those who support you through thick and thin. I love loyal people. I love faithful people. I have friends, family, and staff in my life right now who I know will give me their approval until the day I die.

God has put people in my life who celebrate me and give me the freedom to become who He created me to be. He has put the same types of people in your life—the right people. So don't waste your time trying to win the approval of those who would manipulate you and put you into a box of their design. Your destiny is too great for that. You don't need their approval. You have the approval of almighty God!

Today's Prayer

Father, thank You for the gifts and callings You have placed on my life. I choose to be faithful to You even when other people don't approve. Thank You for Your favor, anointing, and divine connections to fulfill every desire You've placed in my heart. In Jesus' Name. Amen.

Today's Thought

The Scripture tells us that promotion doesn't come from people, promotion comes from the Lord. You may not have the approval of someone "important," but focus on winning the favor of God instead. How do you do that? By being a person of excellence, by having an attitude of faith, by blessing your enemies, and by being good to people.

Stay in Your Own Race

Scripture Reading: John 1

[John] came right out and said, "I am not the Messiah."

JOHN 1:20 NLT

I was watching the Indianapolis 500 on television and admiring the sleek race cars. They're low to the ground, extremely aerodynamic. They are equipped with huge engines that power them at 200 miles per hour down a straightaway. They can take curves at 100 miles an hour. They're quick. They're fast. They're precise.

But in spite of all these strengths, the Indy cars also have weaknesses. They only have room for the driver. They're not that comfortable. The inside is all metal and equipment. No A/C. No stereo. No luxury. Why is that? The Indy cars are designed for a specific purpose, to be the best in their particular race.

Victoria and I have a Suburban SUV that can easily hold eight people comfortably. The trunk area is so big we can put all of our bicycles and luggage back there. The SUV has air-conditioning and a nice stereo system and sits so high you feel like the king of the road.

But if you took our Suburban out on the Indianapolis 500 track, the race cars would run circles around us. The SUV would be lapped again and again. If you tried to take a turn at 100 miles an hour, you would hear the angels say, "Welcome to heaven." The Suburban couldn't handle the

Indy track. The big, comfortable vehicle would be competing in a race it was never designed to run.

On the other hand, if Victoria and I traded our SUV for an Indy race car and tried to use it every day, we might draw a lot of attention—those cars have a lot of sizzle—but I don't know where we'd put the kids or the groceries. If you hit a pothole in one of those things, you'd feel like you were in an earthquake. In a few days we'd be asking for our SUV back.

Each type of car is designed for a specific purpose. The Suburban won't be winning any races on the track at the Indianapolis 500, and the Indy race cars aren't any soccer mom's choice for an everyday vehicle. Still, both types of cars have incredible strengths. The key is to make sure you run them in the right race.

Today, you may be the human version of that Indy car with the speed, the agility, and the looks. If that's you, go for it. Be the best you can be. Run your race. If you're not an Indy-model person, don't feel bad about it. There is nothing wrong with saying, "Those are not my strengths. I'm never going to be that fast. I'm never going to be that agile. I don't look that sporty, but I'm okay with that."

Today's Prayer

Father, thank You for the gifts You have given me. Lead me, guide me, and help me to make the most of them so that I may live according to Your plan and fulfill my destiny. In Jesus' Name. Amen.

Today's Thought

Your race to be the best is yours alone and it is yours to win. God will not measure you against others. He won't judge you according to what a coworker accomplishes, what your neighbor drives, or whether you are as thin as your best friend. God will judge you by what you've done with the gifts He has given you. He'll be interested in how confident and secure you are. Or did you feel insecure and beat yourself up while comparing yourself to others?

Be the Best You!

Scripture Reading: Hebrews 12

Let us run with endurance the race that is set before us, looking unto Jesus, the author and finisher of our faith. HEBREWS 12:1–2 NKJV

I read about a seven-year-old boy, Joey, who was never content with himself. He always was much more impressed with Billy. He walked like Billy and talked like Billy.

Well, Billy didn't like who he was either. He admired Corey. So Billy walked like Corey and talked like Corey. So, Joey was copying Billy, who was copying Corey.

It turned out that Corey had an inferiority complex, too. He was much more impressed with Frankie. So he walked like Frankie and talked like Frankie.

Thus, Joey was copying Billy, who was copying Corey, who was copying Frankie.

You'll never guess what happened next. Frankie wasn't happy with himself either. He admired Joey. So he was walking like Joey, talking like Joey.

All right, let me see if I've got this straight: Joey was copying Billy, who was copying Corey, who was copying Frankie, who was copying *himself*!

This story points out the truth that the people you want to be like, very often, want to be like you. They may admire you just as much as you admire them. So there is nothing wrong with looking up to people. It's good to show respect and admiration. But don't give up your identity for theirs. Run your own race. You have something great to offer.

Today's Prayer

Father, I humbly come to You giving You all that I am. Help me to be the best version of me that I possibly can be. I declare that I won't compete nor compare myself to others. I won't look to the left or to the right but instead I'll keep my eyes on You, Jesus, the Author and Finisher of my faith. In Jesus' Name. Amen.

Today's Thought

When you focus on being who God made you to be, that's when you'll rise higher and position yourself for every spiritual blessing He has in store for you.

Carefully Select Those in Your Circle

Scripture Reading: Mark 5

He did not let anyone follow him except Peter, James and John the brother of James.   MARK 5:37 NIV

When our friends' daughter, whom I'll call Janna, was a teenager, she started dating a boy named Tad after meeting him in a church youth group. Janna's parents were happy that she'd found a boy from a church group. But then they discovered that Tad had been forced to join the group by his parents. They were trying to straighten him out because he had been in so much trouble for violent behavior and drug use. Instead of being a good influence on her, he led Janna astray.

Soon Janna's grades dropped. Her parents caught her lying about where she'd been and whom she'd been with.

It took a long time for Janna's parents to get their daughter back. Years later, she told them that she appreciated how they had stood by her and fought for her. But when they were going through it, Janna couldn't see that her parents were trying to save her from someone who was a very bad influence. Your destiny is too great to reach on your own. God has already arranged supporters to speak faith into you. He has placed others in your path to inspire you, to challenge you, to help you grow and accomplish your dreams. But some people never reach their highest potential because they never get away from the wrong people. Connect with those who understand your destiny, friends who appreciate your uniqueness, and encouragers who can call forth your seeds of greatness.

Your destiny is too great to reach on your own. God has already arranged supporters to speak faith into you. He has placed others in your path to inspire you, to challenge you, to help you grow and accomplish your dreams. But some people never reach their highest potential because they never get away from the wrong people. Connect with those who understand your destiny, friends who appreciate your uniqueness, and encouragers who can call forth your seeds of greatness.

Today's Prayer

Father, help me to choose my relationships wisely. Empower me with boldness to walk away from those who are dragging me down. Let me see clearly and appreciate those who are standing with me, calling forth the seeds of greatness You have placed within me. In Jesus' Name. Amen.

Today's Thought

Not everyone can go where God is taking you. You do not need those who push you down, tell you what you can't become, and never give their approval even when you do well.

God Will Replace the Negative with the Positive

Scripture Reading: Matthew 7

Give not that which is holy unto the dogs, neither cast ye your pearls before swine, lest they trample them under their feet, and turn again and rend you. MATTHEW 7:6 KJV

If you remove the negative people from your life, God will bring positive people into it. Is your inner circle of friends holding you back? Are those closest to you *with* you but not *for* you? If you find that it takes constant effort to win their support and encouragement, they likely don't understand your destiny.

The Bible says not to cast your pearls before swine. You could say your pearl is your gift, your personality. It's who you are. When you get around true friends, people who really believe in you, they won't be jealous of your gifts. They won't constantly question who you are. They won't try to talk you out of your dreams. It will be just the opposite. They'll help you polish your pearls. They'll give you ideas. They'll connect you with people they know. They'll help push you farther along.

Do not waste time with people who don't value your gifts or appreciate what you have to offer. That's casting your pearls before swine. Those closest to you should celebrate who you are and be happy when you succeed. They should believe in the very best of you.

If that doesn't describe those in your inner circle, move them out. You can be nice. You can still be friends from a distance. But your time is too valuable to spend with people who are not 100 percent for you. It's not the quantity of friends that's important; it's the quality of friends. I would rather have two good friends who I know are for me 100 percent than have fifty friends who are only for me 80 percent.

Today's Prayer

Father, help me to see clearly the treasures, the pearls, You have placed within me. Give me wisdom to discern the right relationships you have ordained for me. Thank You for replacing the negative influences in my life with positive ones. In Jesus' Name. Amen.

Today's Thought

When you get around true friends, people who really believe in you, they won't be jealous of your gifts. They won't constantly question who you are. They won't try to talk you out of your dreams. It will be just the opposite. They'll help you polish your pearls, develop your pearls, enhance your pearls, and grow your pearls.

Beware of the Negative and Needy

Scripture Reading: Proverbs 27

As iron sharpens iron, so one person sharpens another.

PROVERBS 27:17 NIV

As a minister, I expect that people in need will come to me. I welcome them and try to help any way I can. That said, there are some people who just keep coming back for more. These negative, needy people constantly dump their problems on your doorstep and expect you to clean them up. They know only one song, and it's sad. After crying with them through eight or nine verses, you realize they don't want to be helped or encouraged. They just want to unload on you. They bask in the attention. They suck the energy right out of you. Spend an hour with them, and you'll feel like you've run a marathon.

Needy people can abuse your kindness. Sometimes you have to put up with their difficulties and love them back to wholeness, but you can't spend your whole life knee-deep in their troubles. You have a God-given destiny to fulfill. I've found that in some cases the best help you can give negative, needy people is not to help them at all. Otherwise, you are just enabling their dysfunction.

Proverbs 27:17 says, "As iron sharpens iron, so one person sharpens another" (NIV). Are your friends making you stronger? Are they challenging you to become a better parent, a better spouse, a better coworker, a better member of your community?

If not, you may have to change where you do business, where you play ball, where you work, where you shop. Your time on this earth is brief and valuable. You have a destiny to fulfill, and you can't make it happen if you are carrying needy and negative people on your back. The solution is found in Mark 5:40, which explains how Jesus "put out" those who doubted Him. Show them the door. Be kind. Be polite. But pull away.

Today's Prayer

Father, thank You for the people You have placed in my life. Help me to see them the way You see them. Help me to be loving and kind, but not manipulated by negative people. Let me help others fulfill Your plan for our lives. In Jesus' Name. Amen.

Today's Thought

God wants us to be different. He's given us different personalities, different strengths, different hobbies, and different looks. He's made us all different so we can sharpen one another and cause each other to rise up higher in life.

Make a Leap Toward Your Destiny

Scripture Reading: Luke 1

When Elizabeth heard Mary's greeting, the baby leaped in her womb, and Elizabeth was filled with the Holy Spirit.　　LUKE 1:41 NIV

In the Scripture, you'll find the story of Elizabeth, who was struggling to have a baby. In those days a lady was despised if she couldn't produce a child. Finally, late in life, Elizabeth conceived. She was so excited about being able to have this baby.

For the first few weeks Elizabeth was just on cloud nine. Her dream was coming to pass. Then, as the delivery date approached, she began to worry. She'd never had a baby before. She was hoping and praying that everything was okay, but three months, four months, five months passed, and she hadn't felt any movement.

The longer it went, the more concerned she became. Then one day there was a knock on her door; an unexpected guest. It was her younger cousin Mary, a teenager. Elizabeth opened the door. Mary gave her a great big hug and said, "Elizabeth! Congratulations! I've heard the great news that you're going to have a baby."

The Scripture says, "When Elizabeth heard Mary's greeting, the baby leaped in her womb."

At that moment Elizabeth knew the child was alive. She knew the promise was going to come to pass!

God has designated people to come into your life to make your baby, your dream, or promise leap. These are positive, faith-filled people who will help bring your dreams to life and your promises to pass.

Mary, of course, was a divine connection. She was ordained by the Creator of the universe to bring hope, faith, and vision into Elizabeth's life. She didn't even have to say anything profound. She just said hello, and the promise within Elizabeth came to life.

God has already lined up your Mary. When you meet the right people, they can simply say "Good morning," and your dreams will leap. That's a supernatural connection.

Mary was pregnant with Jesus, the Son of God. Elizabeth was pregnant with John the Baptist. When the promise in Mary connected with the promise in Elizabeth, there was an explosion of faith. When you meet and mix with the right people, when you connect with big dreamers and big doers, then the promise in you will connect with the promises in them. You will see God show up and do something supernatural in your lives.

Today's Prayer

Father, thank You for bringing people into my life who will confirm what You are doing in me and cause the promise inside of me to leap! I trust that You are ordering my steps and orchestrating my destiny. I give praise and glory for Your faithfulness today and always. In Jesus' Name. Amen.

Today's Thought

If you keep answering the door and your dreams never leap, then you're answering the door for the wrong people. Don't answer the door for a gossiper, a complainer, or a user. Answer the door only for those who inspire you, encourage you, and challenge you to fulfill your God-given destiny.

The Promise Is in You

Scripture Reading: Hebrews 12

Since we are surrounded by so great a cloud of witnesses, let us lay aside every weight, and the sin which so easily ensnares us, and let us run with endurance the race that is set before us, looking unto Jesus, the author and finisher of our faith. HEBREWS 12:1–2 NKJV

Like Elizabeth, you are carrying a promise. You know God has spoken to you, but maybe it's been a long time. Maybe you haven't felt any movement on the inside. Now you're thinking, *Did I hear God right? Is the promise still in me? Am I still going to give birth to this promise?*

I believe God sent me today to be one of your Marys. Concerning that dream or hope of yours you're about to give up on, God is saying, "It will come to pass." The promise is in you. It's alive and well. You may not see anything happening. You may feel that you didn't hear God correctly. But God is still on the throne.

Right now He is arranging things in your favor. What He promised you, He will bring to pass. If you will receive those words by faith, you'll feel something down in your spirit—a kick, a push, a shove. What is that? That's your promise coming alive.

You are a child of the Most High God. You have seeds of greatness on the inside. There is no mistake you've made that is too large for the mercy of God. There is no obstacle too high, no sickness too great, and no dream too big. You and God are a majority.

When you hear words like that, let them take root and you will feel faith springing up. That's your baby, your promise, starting to leap. Before long you'll be convinced that you can achieve all that you desire through God's plan. But if you are to become all He created you to be, you must fill your inner circle with people of vision, faith, and encouragement.

It's not too late. You're not too old. You haven't made too many mistakes. The promise is still alive. Now it's up to you to eliminate those who are holding you back and replace them with those who lift you up. God has already sent them to your door! Let them in, then as iron sharpens iron, you will cut through your challenges and rise higher. I believe and declare that, just like Elizabeth, you will give birth to every promise God put in your heart, and you will become everything God created you to be!

Today's Prayer

Father, thank You that the seeds of greatness inside of me are alive and well. Even when I don't always see it, even when I don't always feel it, I trust that You are at work in me. Thank You for strengthening me and encouraging me to give birth to every promise and fulfill the destiny You have designed for me. In Jesus' Name. Amen.

Today's Thought

God didn't put the promise in somebody else; He put the promise in you. Somebody else may not be able to see what you can see. Don't get discouraged and let them talk you out of your dreams. When God gives you a dream, He gives it to you in seed form. The breaks you need are already in your future. Don't let people talk you out of what God put in your heart.

PART
IV

Travel Light

God Will Settle the Account

Scripture Reading: Hebrews 10

We know the one who said, "I will take revenge. I will pay them back." He also said, "The Lord will judge his own people." It is a terrible thing to fall into the hands of the living God.

HEBREWS 10:30–31 NLT

A woman recently told me that when she was a child, several men abused her. It was very unfair. She grew up confused and ashamed. She thought it was her fault. She didn't trust men. But she would do anything to try to win their approval. That's all she had known. On the inside she was bitter and angry.

For twenty-six years, she did not speak to her father because she blamed him for not protecting her from the abusers. She hated him. Every time she thought about him, she became angry and bitter. But one day she heard me talking about forgiveness. She took it to heart when I said no hurt or offense should keep us from our destinies because when we forgive, it frees us to move forward.

At thirty-six years of age, she traveled to another city and found her father. When he answered the door and saw her, he didn't know what to do. She said, "Dad, what you did by not protecting me was wrong. I've hated you every day of my life, but I can't live with that poison in me anymore. I'm not going to let you continue to mess up my life. I'm forgiving you for everything you've done."

She told me that when she walked away from her father that day, it was like she'd been released from prison. Up to that point she had floundered in life, jumped in and out of relationships, and failed at several jobs. But today, ten years later, she is happily married with three beautiful children. She owns her own business and she is very successful. She says life could not be any better. Her recovery began when she let her hurt go.

Forgive so you can be free. Don't let the person who hurt you keep you in prison. If you let the wrong go, then God will do for you what He did for the woman mentioned above. He'll take what was meant for your harm and He will use it for your advantage. What happened to you may have been painful, but don't waste your pain. God will use that pain to promote you.

You may need some of your accounts settled, too. Maybe somebody stole your childhood, or somebody walked out and left you with a bunch of children to raise, or somebody cheated you in a business deal and you lost a lot of money. You could easily live angry and upset with a chip on your shoulder. Instead, be encouraged. God is a God of justice. He knows every person who hurt you and left you lonely and afraid. Nobody else may have seen it, but He saw it, He knew it wasn't right, and He's saying today, "I'm settling your accounts. I'm making your wrongs right. I'm paying you back not just what you deserve but double."

God said in Isaiah, "Instead of your shame you shall have double honor, and instead of confusion they shall rejoice in their portion. Therefore in their land they shall possess double; everlasting joy shall be theirs" (61:7 NKJV).

Today's Prayer

Father, help me forgive the people who have hurt me. Even if they are gone, I choose to release the pain, bitterness, and offense. Today, I open the door of my heart to receive Your forgiveness and restoration in my own life in return. In Jesus' Name. Amen.

Today's Thought

God never brings you out the same; He always brings you out better. He will make the enemy pay for bringing that injustice into your life. Do your part and let it go. When you choose to forgive, you are handing everything over to God. Today, choose forgiveness and let God be your vindicator. Let Him settle your cases because He promises to repay you double in this life.

God Will Compensate You

Scripture Reading: Matthew 6

Forgive us our debts, as we also have forgiven our debtors.

MATTHEW 6:12 NIV

Sharon hated her father because he ran around on her mother. Sharon didn't have a good childhood. She always resented the fact that her father wasn't faithful and he wasn't there for her growing up. She couldn't stand to be around him.

But do you know when Sharon grew up, she ran around on her husband and broke up her own home? She was not there for her own children. She became exactly what she hated in her father.

That's why it's so important to forgive and let things go. The bitterness, the sin you retain, can produce the same results that hurt you. If you were raised in an abusive environment, if you come from a family filled with anger and dysfunction, instead of becoming bitter and angry, why don't you be the one to put an end to the negative cycle?

You can be the one to make a difference. Are you holding on to anger and unforgiveness and passing poison down to the next generation? Or are you willing to let it go so your family can rise to a new level?

I realize it can be very hard to forgive, especially when someone has hurt you, but God will never ask you to do something without giving you the ability to do it.

Forgiveness is a process. It doesn't happen overnight. You don't snap your fingers and make a hurt go away. That's not realistic. But if you'll continue to have the desire to forgive and ask God to help you, then little by little those negative feelings will fade. One day they won't affect you at all.

When Jesus prayed the Lord's Prayer, He said, "Forgive us our debts, as we also have forgiven our debtors." (Matthew 6:12 NIV) When God talks about debts, He's not just talking about monetary debts. He's talking about the times when people hurt you, the times when people do you wrong. God refers to that as a debt because when you are mistreated, you may feel you are owed something.

Human nature says, "I was wronged. Now I want justice. You mistreated me. Now you've got to pay me back." But the mistake many people make is in trying to collect a debt that only God can pay. The father who allowed his daughter to be abused couldn't give her innocence back to her. Your parents can't make it up to you because you didn't have a loving childhood. Your spouse can't make it up to you for the pain he caused by being unfaithful. Only God can truly do that.

Today's Prayer

Father, I don't want to let bitterness, anger, or offense to have control over my life. Today, I release it all. I release the hurt and pain and I receive Your healing power. Help me forgive others and break the negative cycles of the past as I daily submit myself to You. In Jesus' Name. Amen.

Today's Thought

If you want to be restored and be whole, get on God's payroll. He knows how to make things right. He knows how to bring justice. He'll give you what you deserve. Leave it up to Him. Quit expecting people to make it up to you. They can't give you what they don't have.

Mark It "PAID IN FULL"

Scripture Reading: Matthew 18

The master called the servant in. "You wicked servant," he said, "I canceled all that debt of yours because you begged me to. Shouldn't you have had mercy on your fellow servant just as I had on you?" In anger his master handed him over to the jailers to be tortured, until he should pay back all he owed. "This is how my heavenly Father will treat each of you unless you forgive your brother or sister from your heart."

MATTHEW 18:32–35 NIV

I spoke with a man who was wronged and lost his business. It happened years ago, but he's still mad at the world. He's been with three different companies. He can't keep a job. He is bitter, and he thinks he's owed something. He's waiting to be paid back.

What's the problem? He's on the wrong payroll.

Your attitude should be, *God, You know what I've been through; You've seen every wrong, every hurt, every tear; and God, I will not be bitter, trying to get people to give me what they don't have. You said You would pay me back double for every injustice. So I'm letting all my family, my friends, my coworkers, my neighbors off the hook, and I'm putting my trust, my confidence, my hope in You.*

When you get on God's payroll, He'll make sure you are well compensated. If you would let people off the hook and stop thinking they owe you something, your life would go to a new level. They may have done wrong, and it may have been their fault, but it's not their fault that they can't pay you back.

If you spend your life trying to get from them only what God can give, it will ruin that relationship, and the sad thing is you'll take that same problem into the next and the next and the next relationship after that.

Jesus told a parable about a man who owed ten thousand talents. And the Scripture says, "He could not pay" (Matthew 18:25 AMP). It doesn't say that he didn't want to, but that he could not. He didn't have the means to pay. If you're always looking for people to pay you back for the wrongs they've done, you will lead a life of frustration.

I've seen more than one person go through a bitter divorce, start a new relationship, and then make the mistake of trying to make the new person pay for what the previous spouse did. They're always trying to collect a debt, and it ends up ruining the relationship. Don't punish the person you're married to now for something that happened years ago in another relationship. They can't pay you back. Get on God's payroll.

Sometimes when I'm looking over the bills, I'll see these big red letters that read "PAID IN FULL." Somebody has marked the bill with one of those big rubber stamps. See your accounts, your hurts, as paid in full. Instead of trying to collect from those who hurt you and thinking they owe you, get that big red stamp out and mark the account as "PAID IN FULL."

When you see the person who did you wrong, stamp the account "PAID IN FULL" in your imagination. It's very freeing to say, "Nobody owes me anything. They may have hurt me, they may have done me wrong, they may have stolen my childhood, they may have cheated me out of money, but I'm not looking for people to pay me back. I'm on God's payroll. The good news is, God never misses a payment."

Mark your accounts "PAID IN FULL." Let it go. God will settle your cases. Forgive so you can be free. Forgive so God can pay you back double.

Many airlines now charge you for baggage. It's the same way in life. You can carry around baggage, but it will cost you. You can carry unforgiveness, but it will cost you the day-to-day happiness and joy you desire. You can carry bitterness, but it will cost you peace. You can carry that bag of "They Owe Me Something" around with you, but it's not free. If you do it long enough, there will be a very heavy price. It will keep you from your destiny.

You may say those who hurt you don't deserve to be forgiven. Maybe not, but you do. If you don't forgive them, your Father in heaven can't forgive you. Why don't you let go of the baggage? Why don't you mark some accounts "PAID IN FULL"?

You have to forgive so that you can be free to live each day with happiness in your heart.

Today's Prayer

Father, today I'm choosing to get on Your payroll. I choose to look to You to heal my hurts and right the wrongs done to me. I choose forgiveness and declare that no one owes me anything because You have set me free from my past. In Jesus's Name. Amen.

Today's Thought

If you will let go of the hurts and pains and get on God's payroll, God will settle your case. He will make your wrongs right. He will bring justice into your life. You will get what you deserve, and God will pay you back with double the joy, double the peace, double the favor, and double the victory.

God Will Lift Your Head

Scripture Reading: Numbers 21

Then they journeyed from Mount Hor by the Way of the Red Sea, to go around the land of Edom; and the soul of the people became very discouraged on the way.

And the people spoke against God and against Moses: "Why have you brought us up out of Egypt to die in the wilderness? For there is no food and no water, and our soul loathes this worthless bread."

So the LORD sent fiery serpents among the people, and they bit the people; and many of the people of Israel died.

NUMBERS 21:4–6 NKJV

The people of Israel were headed toward the Promised Land, but they "became very discouraged on the way" (Numbers 21:4 NKJV). What's interesting is God was leading them, so it's not like they were actually lost. Yet since they were so easily discouraged, they felt lost.

Little by little, they were worn down. They were good people who loved the Lord. They had seen great victories in the past. Deep down they knew they were headed toward the Promised Land, but over time they lost their passion for life.

Finally they said, "Forget it. Let's just go back to Egypt. It's never going to work."

What happened? They didn't pass the discouragement test. One of the happiness tests you will have to face on a regular basis is the test of over-coming discouragement. No matter how successful you are or how many victories you've had in the past, sooner or later there will be an opportunity to give up your happiness and become discouraged.

I see too many people who've allowed life to wear them down. They once were joyful. They walked with a spring in their steps. They greeted each day with excitement. But over time, they've allowed their happiness to give way to heaviness. Just like a dark cloud, it follows them everywhere they go. Unless they learn how to pass the discouragement test, it will keep them from God's best.

You may face problems and setbacks, but remember, God is still leading the way. He has given us the strength to be where we are with a good attitude. When that discouraging spirit comes knocking on the door, you don't have to answer. Just say, "No, thanks. I'm keeping my joy. I know God is in control of my life. He will allow me to go where I'm supposed to be."

There will be opposition on the way to your destiny. It may take longer than you had hoped. It may be more difficult than you'd thought. You can easily feel discouraged and think it will never work out, whatever the challenge might be. But you have to realize, on the other side of that discouragement awaits a new level of your destiny. When you pass the test, there will always be a promotion.

If you are to become everything God has created you to be, you must be willing to say, "I have come too far to stop now. It may be tough. It may be taking a long time. I may not understand it, but I do know this: My God is still on the throne, and what He promised, He will bring to pass."

Have a made-up mind, and resolve that no matter what comes your way, no matter how long it takes or how impossible it looks, you are in it for the long haul. You will not lose your passion. You will pass these discouragement tests. Your victory is already on the way.

Like the people of Israel, you are right next door to your promised land. Your due season is right around the corner—that breakthrough, that dream coming to pass, meeting the right person, and overcoming that obstacle.

God has already put it on His schedule. He has already set the time and the date to make it happen.

Today's Prayer

Father, today I shake off discouragement, I shake off frustration, I shake off worry and fear. I trust that where I am is where I am supposed to be. I trust that You are leading and guiding me into the best plan for my life. In Jesus' Name. Amen.

Today's Thought

Now is not the time to be discouraged. Now more than ever is the time to be a believer. It's the time to stay in faith.

Take a Step of Faith

Scripture Reading: John 5

Jesus said to him, "Get up! Pick up your mat and walk." At once the man was cured; he picked up his mat and walked.

JOHN 5:8–9 NIV

I see too many people becoming discouraged these days. They start out fine, but then they hit a setback. Instead of shaking it off and creating a new vision, they let life wear them down and they lose their passion. They end up settling for less than God's best.

In the Scripture there is a man who did this. We are never given his name, but he was one of the many sick people at the pool of Bethesda. He'd been sick for thirty-eight years. When Jesus saw him, He realized he had been ill for a long time and asked him, "Do you want to be made well?" (John 5:6 NKJV).

The man said he couldn't get well because there was no one to put him into the healing waters of the pool and he was too weak to make it on his own. Jesus told him to get up, pick up his mat, and walk.

The man had to make a decision right then and there. Could he do what he had never done before? I'm sure there was a battle going on in his mind. There were strongholds that had been there for years that had convinced him he would never be better. He could have made plenty of excuses, but he did not offer any.

He dared to take a step of faith.

Life may have weakened and discouraged you over time, but God is saying to you what He said to this man. If you want to be healed, stand up. Believe you can go places you've never been before. Stretch into a new way of thinking. Stretch into a greater vision for the possibilities in your life.

Today's Prayer

Father, thank You for Your Word, which lights my way and builds my faith. Today I declare that I trust You and I will take a step of faith in obedience to You. Thank You for helping me let go of limiting, self-defeating mindsets so I can stretch forward in to the new levels You have in store for me. In Jesus' Name. Amen.

Today's Thought

Where you are is not where God wants you to stay. Just because your dream hasn't happened in the past doesn't mean that it cannot happen in the future. If you join in agreement with God and stand up, so to speak, God will have new seasons of promotion and increase coming your way.

God Has a Plan

Scripture Reading: Jeremiah 29

"I know the plans I have for you," declares the LORD, *"plans to prosper you and not to harm you, plans to give you hope and a future."*

JEREMIAH 29:11 NIV

A young lady named June lost both her legs in an accident. She was naturally distraught and depressed. For a time, she didn't think she had any reason to be alive. She didn't see anything good in her future. But I love what she did. She would refer to Jeremiah 29:11 and say, "God, even though I don't have any plans and I'm too overwhelmed to see anything good, I know You have plans and they are good to give me a future and a hope."

If you ever find yourself overwhelmed and you don't see anything good in your future, I would encourage you to do what June did and just get in agreement with God and say, "God, I know You've got a good plan. You've got a purpose for me. You've got brighter days in store for me up ahead."

Sometimes when we're being tested by discouragement, it seems God is silent. We pray and we don't hear anything. We read the Scripture and still come away feeling like God is a million miles away. But remember, this is a test. When you're in school, teachers never talk during tests. They stand up at the front of the room very quietly, just watching all the students taking the exam.

The teachers have been preparing you in the days and weeks prior to the test. Often, they've put in extra hours making sure everyone has the opportunity to succeed. On test day, they want to see if you've learned the lessons. They know that you have the information you need. They know you're prepared. You're ready. Now all you've got to do is put into practice what you've learned.

God is not mad at you when He is silent. He has not forsaken you. His silence is a sign that He has great confidence in you. He knows you have what it takes. He knows you will come through the test victoriously, or He would not have permitted you to be tested.

The key is to remain upbeat and not to be discouraged or bitter. Put into practice what you've learned. Stay in faith. Hang on to your happiness. Treat others kindly. Be a blessing. If you do that, you will pass the test and flourish in a new season. God will bring things out of you that you didn't even know were in you. Understand, if you don't allow the enemy to discourage you, one of his greatest weapons has been lost.

Today is a new day. God is breathing new hope into your heart and new vision into your spirit. He is the Glory and the lifter of our heads. Look up with a fresh vision, and God will do for you what He promised the future King David. He will lift you out of the pit. He will set your feet on a rock. He will put a new song in your heart. You won't drag through life defeated and depressed. You will soar through life full of joy, full of faith, full of victory.

Today's Prayer

Father, thank You for the good plan You have for my life. Even when I don't understand things, I choose to put my hope and trust in You. Help me pass the discouragement test and live in the joy and victory You have planned. In Jesus' Name. Amen.

Today's Thought

God works the same way as your teachers here on earth. When He is silent, don't assume He has left you. He is right there with you during the test. The silence means only that God has prepared you, and now He is watching to see if you have learned. He would not give you the test unless He knew you were ready.

God Has the Solution

Scripture Reading: Matthew 5

*Your Father in heaven . . . makes His sun rise on the evil and on the good,
and sends rain on the just and on the unjust.*

MATTHEW 5:45 NKJV

It's one thing to know that you are entering a challenging season and facing a test of discouragement. You can mentally prepare for those trials. But what about the difficulties you do not see coming? What about life's earthquakes, tsunamis, and tornadoes—the unexpected illnesses, sudden deaths, divorces, and other tragedies and crises that catch us totally unprepared and off guard? They can be overwhelming, even devastating. They come out of nowhere and suddenly our lives are turned upside down.

Our family has had its share of unexpected hits, but probably the most shocking was the mail bomb that exploded and injured my sister Lisa in January 1990. The package contained a pipe bomb packed with seven-inch nails. Lisa opened it in her church office, holding it in her lap. Miraculously, she was not seriously injured. She had minor burns and cuts. To this day, we don't know who sent the package addressed to our father.

Lisa was just opening the morning's mail, a daily routine. Her life was spared. She did not suffer long-term injuries. Yet you can imagine how it turned her life upside down. We were all affected to some degree, but she dealt with both the physical and, even more, the emotional impact for many, many years. In the end, the power of her faith pulled her through. She wrote about it in her book *You Are Made for More!*

We all have to deal with unexpected tragedies and trauma. Being a believer doesn't exempt you from life's turbulent times.

The Scripture says that the Father "sends rain on the just and on the unjust." When you find yourself facing a crisis, it's easy to give up your happiness, panic, and fall apart. But you have to realize that crisis is not a surprise to God. It may be unexpected to us, but God knows the end from the beginning. God has solutions to problems that we haven't even had. And God would not have allowed the difficulty unless He had a divine purpose for it.

You have to remember, you are in a controlled environment. It may seem that your circumstances are out of control, but the Creator of the universe is in complete control. He has you in the palm of His hand.

Nothing can happen to you without God's permission. In fact, God is even in control of our enemies. The Scripture talks about how God caused Pharaoh to harden his heart and not let the people go. Notice that God *caused* him to be difficult. Why was that? So God could show His power in extraordinary ways.

God's purpose in crises is not just to show us His power but to show other people what He can do. If you will view that adversity as an opportunity for God to display His greatness, God will use you as an example. He wants your neighbors to say, "How in the world did she make it? The medical report said 'impossible,' but look at her today. She's as strong and healthy as can be." Or, "He was laid off at the worst possible time, but look at him now. He has an even better job than before."

God wants to turn your test into a testimony. That's why God will allow you to face adversity. Being a believer doesn't make you immune to difficulty. But God promises if you will stay in faith, He will take what was meant for your harm and use it not only to your advantage but also to display His greatness to other people.

It is true that the rain falls on the just and the unjust. But here is the difference. For the just, for the believers—that's you and me—the Scripture says no weapon formed against us will ever prosper. It doesn't say that challenges will never take form. Instead, it says you may face difficulties, but because you're a child of the Most High God, they will not prosper against you. They will not get the best of you. You will get the best of them. God will bring you out better off than you were before.

Today's Prayer

Father, I thank You for Your hand of protection and provision upon me. Help me deal with the unexpected challenges by remembering that You are still on the throne and by understanding that every setback is a setup for You to show Your greatness in and through me. In Jesus' Name. Amen.

Today's Thought

When something unexpected happens, instead of falling apart and panicking, expect God to show up and turn the situation around. Expect God's favor. Expect His supernatural power.

Just Wait and Let God Take Care of It for You

Scripture Reading: Romans 8

We know that all things work together for good to them that love God, to them who are the called according to his purpose.

ROMANS 8:28 KJV

A dog bit a man on his walk one day. He went to the doctor and discovered the dog had rabies. When he learned he would have to have a series of painful antirabies shots, the man went into a rage.

The doctor left him to prepare the shots. When he came back, he found the man writing out a list. He thought his patient was writing a will.

"Sir, it's not that bad," the doctor said. "You won't die from this."

"This is not my will," his patient said. "This is a list of all the people I'm going to bite."

I know people like that. They encounter some turbulence, and they become mad at the world. They spread poison everywhere they go. Don't let that be you. When unexpected challenges appear, your attitude should be: *This, too, shall pass. God will help me handle this. It's just another step on the way to my divine destiny.*

Joseph in the Bible had to have this attitude. He was constantly dealing with unexpected difficulties. He never expected his own brothers to throw him into a pit and sell him into slavery. He could have said, "God, that's not fair. I thought You put a dream in my heart."

Instead, Joseph understood this principle. He knew God would take care of the weeds, so he just kept being his best. He never expected Potiphar's wife to lie about him and have him thrown into prison. He never expected the cell mate he had helped to turn his back on him.

Joseph was hit with one bad break after another. He could have turned bitter and angry. Instead, he kept being his best, and he ended up second in command of a whole nation.

"You intended to harm me, but God intended it for good to accomplish what is now being done, the saving of many lives" (Genesis 50:20 NIV).

You may be in a time of turbulence right now. Your situation may look very difficult, but I'm here to tell you, "This, too, shall pass."

God did not bring you this far to fail you now. It may be rocky. But God is saying, "I still have a way. I am Jehovah-Jireh, the Lord Your Provider. I'm Jehovah-Rapha, the Lord Your Healer. I am El Shaddai, the God Who Is More Than Enough."

If that unexpected crisis you are facing could stop you, be assured God would have never allowed it to happen. If that sudden challenge could have kept you from your destiny, the Most High God would not have permitted it.

If you're alive and breathing, you can still become everything God has created you to be. Don't allow a crisis to steal your joy or keep you from pressing forward.

Today's Prayer

Father, thank You for Your strength and peace during the storms of life. When unexpected challenges come, help me to not be bitter but to turn to you instead. I trust that You are making a way where there seems to be no way as I keep doing my best with what You've placed in my hands. In Jesus' Name. Amen.

Today's Thought

Nothing in life is wasted. God will use even times of turbulence to your advantage. You've heard the saying "Bad things happen to good people." That is true. But it's also true that good people overcome bad things and come out better off than they were before. God will turn your test into a testimony.

Don't Have a Critical Spirit

Scripture Reading: Titus 1

To the pure, all things are pure, but to those who are corrupted and do not believe, nothing is pure. In fact, both their minds and consciences are corrupted.   TITUS 1:15 NIV

A couple moved into a new neighborhood, and one morning while they were eating breakfast, the wife looked out the window and saw her neighbor hanging wash on the line to dry. She noticed the wash was dingy and dirty. She said to her husband, "That neighbor lady doesn't know how to wash. Her clothes aren't clean. I wonder if she's even using any detergent."

Day after day went by and she would make the same comments: "I can't believe the neighbor doesn't know how to wash. I can't believe they wear those dingy-looking clothes."

A few weeks later the woman looked out the window and the clothes were as clean and bright as could be. She was so surprised. She called her husband in and said, "Look, honey, I can't believe it. She finally learned how to wash. I wonder what happened."

The husband smiled and said, "Honey, I got up early this morning and cleaned our window."

How dirty the neighbor's clothes appear depends on how clean your window is. The Scripture says, "To the pure, all things are pure." If you can't see anything in a positive light, if you drive up and down the freeway and see only the potholes, if you see only the scratch in the floor and never the amazing house, if you see only what your boss does wrong and never what he does right, then my advice is to clean your window.

The problem is not with everyone else; instead, you have an internal problem. It's like the man who had an accident driving to work. He got out and said, "Lady, why don't you learn how to drive? You're the fourth person who has hit me today."

At some point look in the mirror and say, "Maybe I'm the one who needs to change. If I'm always critical, maybe I've developed a habit of seeing the bad rather than seeing the good. If I'm always skeptical, maybe I've trained myself to be cynical and sarcastic rather than believing the best. If I'm always finding fault, maybe my filter is dirty. Maybe I've become judgmental and condemning instead of giving people the benefit of the doubt."

This is especially important in relationships. You can train yourself to see people's strengths or you can train yourself to see their weaknesses. You can focus on the things you like about your spouse and magnify the good qualities, or you can focus on the things you don't like and magnify the less-desirable characteristics that annoy you.

This is why some relationships are in such trouble. People have developed a habit of being critical. They can't see anything good. I heard about a man who asked his wife to make him two eggs, one fried and one scrambled. She made them and put them on a plate. When he saw the meal, he shook his head.

"What did I do wrong now?" she asked. "That's exactly what you asked for."

"I knew this would happen," he said. "You fried the wrong egg."

Some people have become so critical-minded that no matter what is done for them, it's not right. They never see the good their spouses are doing. They've forgotten the reasons they fell in love. It's because they're magnifying the wrong things.

Start focusing on your spouse's good qualities. Your entire outlook is poisoned when you operate out of a critical spirit. You won't communicate properly. You won't want to do things together. It will affect you in every area. You have to make a shift. Start appreciating that person's strengths and learn to downplay the weaknesses.

Everyone has faults and habits that can get on your nerves. The key is to recognize what you are magnifying. You are magnifying the wrong thing when you let the critical spirit take over. That's when you'll start complaining that the wrong egg was fried. There are relationships today where two good people are married. They have great potential, but a critical spirit is driving them apart. When you are critical you start nagging: "You never take out the trash. You never talk to me. You're always late."

People respond to praise more than they respond to criticism. The next time you want your husband to mow the lawn, instead of nagging, "Why don't you ever mow the lawn, you lazy thing?" say instead, "Did I ever tell you that when you mow the lawn, you look really good out there, and when your muscles bulge out of your shirt and that sweat drips down your face, you look so handsome and so attractive?"

You praise him like that, and he'll mow the lawn every day!

Today's Prayer

Father, help me to not have a critical spirit but to always see the best in people and circumstances. Let my words be words of life so that I can empower others the way you empower me. In Jesus' Name. Amen.

Today's Thought

If you struggle in this area of being critical, make a list of the qualities you like about your spouse. Write down the good things he or she does. He may not be a great communicator, but he's a hard worker. Write it down. She may have some weaknesses, but she's a great mother. She's smart. She's fun. Put that on your list and go over it every day.

Give the Benefit of the Doubt

Scripture Reading: Proverbs 15

The soothing tongue is a tree of life, but a perverse tongue crushes the spirit. PROVERBS 15:4 NIV

Most of the time if someone is not up to par, there is a very good reason. We don't know what's going on behind closed doors. We don't know the heartache or the pain the person may be pushing down. Maybe they are doing the best they can to just keep it together. The last thing they need is for someone to dump another load on them. God puts people like that in our lives not to be judged, condemned, or criticized. God puts them there so we can help love them back into wholeness.

Where are the healers? Where are the sensitive people who recognize when someone is hurting? Who will step up and say, "I can tell you're stressed out. I can tell you're not feeling up to par. Is there anything I can do to help? Can I pray for you? Can I buy you dinner? Can I come over and encourage you?"

Let's stop judging people and start healing people.

I was in a long grocery store checkout line of about nine people, and the young woman running the cash register seemed to be stressed out. She was very short with people and some of them were short with her in return. She made no bones about the fact that she did not want to be working.

The mood was tense and only worsened when she had a problem with her register. She had to call the manager, causing further delays. Then she needed a price check on someone's groceries. It was taking so long my bananas were no longer green!

Customers in line were grumbling about her bad attitude, which seemed to only make her ruder. The checkout clerk was wrong. She should not have been rude to the customers, but her actions were so out of line I knew something else was bothering her.

There was obviously a deeper problem than work stress. I decided to be part of the solution rather than part of the problem.

When my turn finally came to check out, I smiled and encouraged her.

"Hey, I can tell you're stressed out about something and people are aggravating you, but I'm here to tell you that whatever the problem is, it will work out. Everything will be all right. God has you in the palm of His hand. He knows what you are going through. He has the solution."

Big tears streamed down her cheeks. At first she struggled to say anything, biting her lip, but then the words poured out.

"My baby is in St. Joseph's, the hospital, and I've been so worried," she said. "Then yesterday, my husband was laid off. I don't know how we're going to make it."

I've been known to offer a prayer in all sorts of situations, but this was my first time in the grocery checkout line.

"Let me pray for you," I said to her.

Right there in Express Lane 2, we prayed. When we finished, the lady in line behind me walked around and gave the checkout clerk a big hug.

A man back in the line said, "My good friend is the head nurse at that hospital. I'm going to call her and ask her to go check on your baby."

The whole atmosphere changed because once we heard her story, we understood. Instead of looking at her with a critical view, we looked at her with the eyes of love. Instead of responding to her rudeness, we responded to her sadness and concern. We understood and we empathized after realizing why she was so uptight.

Before I left, she said, "You'll never know what this has meant to me."

Today's Prayer

Father, help me give the people around me the benefit of the doubt. Help me see others through eyes of love and compassion. Let my words be words of life to lift the fallen and help the hurting. In Jesus' Name. Amen.

Today's Thought

Today, listen to your heart. Take time to be still and quiet before the Lord. Allow Him to teach you what to say. As you submit your words and ways to Him, He will direct your path.

Help the Hurting

Scripture Reading: Matthew 7

By their fruit you will recognize them.

MATTHEW 7:16 NIV

When I was a boy attending my father's church, there was a member of the congregation we called "the dancing man." This member of the congregation was in his thirties, and he was always dancing during the service. As soon as the music began, he'd be up on his feet, hands in the air, dancing without inhibition.

I was ten years old or so and I'd sit with my friends making fun of the dancing man. We just thought he was so odd. We would even look for him before the service so we'd know where to get a good view of him dancing. We'd do a play-by-play when the music started. "There go his hands! There go his legs!"

We just couldn't understand why he was always so excited, why he was dancing. My father, being the man he was, called the dancing man up on the platform one Sunday and asked him to tell his story.

You can believe our young ears were tuned in. Finally, we were going to find out what made him so strange, why he danced all the time in church. Our attitudes, and our perspectives, changed as he spoke.

He explained that he'd never known his father and that his mother committed suicide at an early age. He'd grown up angry and bitter, with no direction and no purpose.

He'd always felt lost and alone until he found Lakewood Church, he said. In our church, he'd felt a sense of belonging for the first time. He felt loved and supported. That encouragement helped him turn his life around. He found a good job and married a woman who loved him. My father's church gave him the foundation that his life had lacked, something he could build upon and draw strength from.

"When I think about all God has done for me, I just can't be still. My arms go up in the air," he said. "When the music starts, my legs just go to dancing. I'm so happy I've just got to give God praise."

When my friends and I heard his story, we felt about two inches tall. We never made fun of him again. We learned that when you imagine walking in somebody's shoes, when you hear their entire story, you gain a new and deeper perspective.

Could it be the person you've been judgmental toward has a good reason for the way he is? Maybe he has an addiction. You're tempted to write him off, to be critical, but have you imagined walking in his shoes? Do you know how he was raised? Do you know what battles he has fought?

Most of the time we don't know all the facts about the people we judge and criticize. Even if they are in the wrong, God did not put us here to condemn them. They need our mercy, our forgiveness, and our understanding to get back on the right track. Being hard and critical doesn't bring healing. We aren't lifting people up. We just push them farther down.

Today's Prayer

Father, today I let go of preconceived ideas about the people in my life. I choose love. I choose understanding. I choose mercy, forgiveness, and compassion to help others move forward on the road to victory. In Jesus' Name. Amen.

Today's Thought

The Scripture says people will know true Christians by their fruit. Others are watching us to see how Christians live their faith, and one of the best witnesses we could have is to simply be good to people. If you'll get up every day and focus on how you can be a blessing and not just on how you can be blessed, God will meet your own needs as you meet others' needs. God will meet all your needs in abundance.

Be the One to Lighten the Load

Scripture Reading: Proverbs 11

A generous person will prosper; whoever refreshes others will be refreshed.
PROVERBS 11:25 NIV

Teddy was a fifth grader struggling in school. He wouldn't participate. He was moody and hard to deal with. His teacher, Ms. Thompson, always said that she loved all of her students, but later she would admit that she hadn't cared for Teddy at first. She couldn't understand why he was so unmotivated and unwilling to learn.

At Christmas the students brought Ms. Thompson presents that she would open in front of the class. Most were wrapped in fancy holiday paper with sparkling bows, but Teddy's present was wrapped in brown paper from a grocery bag. When she opened it up, out fell a very plain-looking bracelet that had half the rhinestones missing, plus a bottle of cheap perfume, half of which was gone.

Some of the students giggled at Teddy's present, but Ms. Thompson hushed them and acted pleased, dabbing on some of the perfume and placing the bracelet around her wrist. She then held it up and said, "Oh, it's so beautiful."

After class Teddy came up to the teacher and said very quietly, "Ms. Thompson, that bracelet looks as beautiful on you as it did on my mother. And with that perfume you smell just like she did."

After Teddy left, Ms. Thompson rushed to the files to find out more about his family. She found the paperwork. It read: "First grade: Teddy shows promise but has very poor home situation. Second grade: Teddy could do better but mother is seriously ill. Third grade: Teddy is a good boy but distracted. Mother died this year. Fourth grade: Teddy is a slow learner. Father shows no sign of interest in him."

After reading the reports, Ms. Thompson wiped away the tears and said, "God, please forgive me."

The next morning when the students went to class, they had a new teacher. You see, Ms. Thompson had become a new person. She'd exchanged her critical eyes for the eyes of love. She'd come to understand why Teddy was so distracted and unmotivated.

She made the boy her personal project, showing him love and encouragement, tutoring and mentoring him. The empathy and acceptance of Ms. Thompson changed the course of Teddy's life. Years after he'd moved on to high school, the teacher received a letter from her former student Teddy.

"Ms. Thompson, thank you for all you did for me in grade school. I'm about to graduate from high school second in my class."

Four years later, another letter: "Ms. Thompson, thanks again for all of your encouragement years ago. I'm about to graduate from college first in my class."

Then came one final letter: "Ms. Thompson, thank you. I am now Dr. Teddy. I just graduated from medical school. Also, I'm about to be married, and I wanted to see if you would come to the wedding. I'd like to seat you where my mother would have been if she were still alive."

What a difference it makes in your happiness and the joy of others when you take time to hear the stories of others. It's easy to be critical. It's easy to write people off. But I'm convinced, like Ms. Thompson, if you will make an effort to find out what they're all about, it will be a lot easier to show mercy.

Make sure you see people through eyes of love, not eyes of judgment. Don't be critical and don't write people off. Give them the benefit of the doubt. Go the extra mile. Consider that they might be going through incredible difficulties and they are doing the best they can. Be a person who helps lighten the load.

All it takes for some is just one person stepping up or lending a hand. You can be the Ms. Thompson in someone's life. You can be the difference-maker. Take an interest in that coworker who is so discouraged. Find out what's going on with that relative who has lost his passion.

You can be the catalyst for change. If you see people through eyes of love and do not judge them, you will live as a healer, lifting the fallen, restoring the broken. Let me assure you, when you help others come up higher, God will make sure you come up higher. He will pour out His blessings and His favor.

Today's Prayer

Father, thank You for Your grace and mercy in my life. I surrender every area of my life to You and invite You to use me to help others. Teach me to be generous with my time, resources, and encouragement so I can refresh and strengthen others always. In Jesus' Name. Amen.

Today's Thought

Today, look for someone to be a blessing to. As you step out and refresh others, as you live a life of generosity, you will be refreshed and experience God's blessing in your own life in return. Refreshing someone can be as simple as a smile or an encouraging word. Don't wait until you feel like doing it; that day may never come! Do it because the Scripture tells us to. Do it because it blesses the Lord.

PART
V

Laugh Often

Laughter Heals

Scripture Reading: John 15

As the Father has loved me, so have I loved you. Now remain in my love. If you keep my commands, you will remain in my love, just as I have kept my Father's commands and remain in his love. I have told you this so that my joy may be in you and that your joy may be complete.

JOHN 15:9–11 NIV

Many people are too stressed to have fun. They need to restore balance. All work and no play is not healthy. Developing a sense of humor and looking for opportunities to laugh can make a big difference in the quality of your life. You may not be a jovial person by nature. God made us all unique. But I recommend training yourself to laugh as often as possible.

Medical science is catching on to the benefits of laughter as therapy for patients and to improve patient-caregiver relationships. There is even a "humor-in-hospitals movement," which includes using "clown care units" to entertain patients and improve their moods. Some hospitals now have "humor carts," which are wheeled into patients' rooms with funny-movie DVDs, cartoon books, games, and funny props to provide comic relief from stress and pain.

St. Joseph Medical Center in Houston, where I live, had one of the first "humor rooms" in the country. These are special rooms set aside where patients and their families can laugh and have fun without disturbing others. The St. Joseph staff found that visits to the humor room led to many patients leaving the hospital sooner because it helped relieve pain and other symptoms.

Another hospital had a humor program in its pediatrics ward. When there was a shortage of beds, a depressed seventy-year-old man with cancer was put in the pediatric ward temporarily. He felt so much better after staying there, he asked to be with the kids the next time he was admitted.

I heard about another hospital that takes some of its long-term patients to a park several hours a week so they can watch children playing. The original purpose was to get them out of the hospital and into a more relaxing environment. But doctors discovered that watching the children play and hearing them laugh stimulated the body's natural healing process.

Just watching and listening to children at play helped change the patients' outlooks and they recovered more quickly. If just watching children laugh and play helps bring healing and joy and a better attitude, imagine what laughing and playing yourself can do for you.

Today's Prayer

Father, thank You for the healing power of laughter. Help me let go of stress and learn to be joyful each and every day. Give me wisdom to plan my days so that I can rejuvenate my being and give You glory in everything I do. In Jesus' Name. Amen.

Today's Thought

As believers, you and I are supposed to be the happiest people on earth. Everywhere we go, we should be so full of joy that we brighten their day.

Fill Your Mouth with Laughter

Scripture Reading: Job 8

He will yet fill your mouth with laughter and your lips with shouts of joy.
JOB 8:21 NIV

I heard a story about Joey Grimaldi, a comedian in the early 1800s who kept people laughing during his forty-year career. Joey was known to turn angry mobs into applauding audiences, but he wasn't such a happy man himself. He was a workaholic. He felt pressured to always be funnier and funnier. He was a perfectionist, never satisfied with his routines or his success.

Later in his life, he became ill, but he kept performing. He went to a doctor he'd never seen before. Joey had aged because of overwork and self-imposed stress. This doctor didn't recognize Joey as the famed comedian. After examining him, the physician told his new patient that there was no medical reason for his illness, other than stress from overwork and possible depression.

"I don't know what you do for a living, but I suggest you just take some time off from work and relax. Go see that great comedian Joey Grimaldi who's in town this week. I hear he's hilarious, and laughter will do you some good."

Joey looked at the doctor and sadly replied, "But Doctor, I *am* Joey Grimaldi." A few weeks later, in March 1823, amid the applause and laughter of a packed house, Joey collapsed and died from exhaustion. Sadly, he could make others laugh, but he never took the time to laugh himself. Don't let that be you.

Today's Prayer

Father, thank You for filling me with joy unspeakable and full of glory! I declare that today is a new day. I shake off the old, I shake off stress and pressure and I set my hope in You. Help to laugh, to lighten my load, and enjoy the good life You have arranged for me. In Jesus' Name. Amen.

Today's Thought

I'm sure you've known stressed-out people like Joey Grimaldi who seem to age rapidly because of their challenges. When we're stressed and too serious and grumpy, the chemicals that God designed to keep us young, to relieve stress, to reduce blood pressure, to make our immune systems stronger, sit unused. God has given us everything we need to live healthy and whole lives, but it's up to us to tap into His provision through laughter and seeing the humor in life.

Humor for Your Health

Scripture Reading: Psalm 126

Now, GOD, do it again—bring rains to our drought-stricken lives so those who planted their crops in despair will shout hurrahs at the harvest, so those who went off with heavy hearts will come home laughing, with armloads of blessing. PSALM 126:4–6 THE MESSAGE

Among its other medical benefits, laughter triggers the right side of the brain, which helps creativity and decision making. When you have a good laugh, you activate the body's natural tranquilizers that calm you and help you sleep better. Many people today suffer from insomnia, but maybe laughing more would help them relax and rest.

One poor lady, Virginia, was constantly taking tranquilizers because she hadn't been able to sleep well for so long. But she took the tranquilizers so often they hardly helped. Virginia tried different diets, doctors, and herbs, too, but nothing seemed to work.

Then a doctor gave her a very unusual prescription. He said, "Every night before you go to bed, watch something funny—a funny movie, a funny video, a funny sitcom—something that makes you laugh."

Virginia followed his advice night after night. She slept better and better. Finally, she was totally off her sleep medications and snoozing every night like a baby.

What happened? Virginia needed man-made tranquilizers because she wasn't releasing God's natural tranquilizers. Maybe you, too, would feel better if you lightened up and laughed more often. It could be that your headaches, backaches, migraines, chronic pain, or fatigue might ease if you played, laughed, and enjoyed life more.

Today's Prayer

Father, thank You that I am fearfully and wonderfully made. Thank You for equipping me with the ability to stimulate my natural tranquilizers for better rest and optimal health. Help me laugh and enjoy life more often so I can embrace the fullness of the blessing You have for me. In Jesus Name. Amen.

Today's Thought

When you have a heavy heart, when life deals you a difficult blow, God wants to turn things around in your favor. Not only does He want to bring you out, but He wants to bring you out with a smile and better off than you were before. He wants to give you victory and fill you with armloads of blessings! God wants to overwhelm you with His goodness. He wants you to feel as if you are living in a dream.

Keep a Cheerful Heart

Scripture Reading: Proverbs 17

A cheerful heart is good medicine, but a crushed spirit dries up the bones.
PROVERBS 17:22 NIV

A doctor friend told me about a woman with a severe case of fibromyalgia, a disorder of unknown origins that causes widespread and chronic pain throughout the body. This woman spent many hours in bed suffering. She also had chronic fatigue and was very depressed.

Her doctor treated the pain with medications, but he felt the pills were treating only the symptoms and not the cause. In talking to her, the doctor realized how depressed she was. Then he asked her an interesting question: "How long has it been since you've had a good, hearty laugh?"

The lady had to think about it a moment.

"Doctor," she said, "I haven't laughed that way in more than thirty years, since I was a child."

"Well, here's your prescription," he said. "Go watch every funny movie you can find. Go read every humorous book you can get your hands on, and laugh as much as you possibly can."

She followed his prescription, and little by little, her joy returned. The pain subsided. Her energy was restored. Three months later she returned to the doctor for a checkup. The moment she walked in, he could see the difference. There was a sparkle in her eye, a spring in her step, a smile on her face.

"Doctor," she said, "I've never felt so good in all my life."

In the months that followed, she continued to laugh more and more. Her laughter cleansed her body of whatever was causing her pain.

Today's Prayer

Father, thank You for giving me a cheerful heart and helping me laugh every day. Thank You for the gift of laughter that is good medicine for my mind and body; strengthening and empowering me to live happy, healthy, and whole. In Jesus' Name. Amen.

Today's Thought

Let me ask you what the doctor asked her: How long has it been since you've had a good, hearty laugh? A day? A week? A month? A year? Ten years? Make sure you're taking your medicine.

God Has Fixed the Fight for Your Health

Scripture Reading: Psalm 2

He Who sits in the heavens laughs.

PSALM 2:4 AMP

I know when I've had a hard, pressure-filled day because I end up with a backache down the center of my spine. I know it's from tension. To relieve that pain, I'll go play with my children. They always make me laugh. Or I'll watch something funny on television.

Invariably, after a few minutes of laughing, that pain is totally gone. It's just like I had a good massage but cheaper. The medicine of laughter will save you money. No more buying sleeping pills, tranquilizers, or antidepressants!

Psalm 2:4 says that God sits in the heavens and laughs. Can you envision that? Right now God is on the throne. He's not mad. He's not worried about the economy. He's not upset with you and me. God is on the throne, full of joy.

Psalm 37:13 explains that why He's laughing because He can see the enemy is about to be defeated. In other words, the reason God laughs is because He knows the end of the story. He knows the final outcome. The good news is, you and I win. God always causes us to triumph!

It's just like we are in a fixed fight. The outcome is predetermined by God. Imagine you knew who'd win the Super Bowl before the kickoff. No matter how far behind the eventual winner fell, no matter how bad it looked for them, you wouldn't worry. You had inside information. You knew the final outcome.

That's what God is saying: When it gets tough and things don't look like they'll work out, you can laugh by faith, knowing that God has already written the final chapter. God has already recorded the victory in your favor.

In famine, when it gets tough, look that trouble in the face and laugh and say, "I know the outcome. God has destined me to win. He's already put my name on the trophy. He's already seen me standing on the podium as a winner."

God gave Abraham a promise that he would father a child. In the natural it was impossible. He was much too old. But the first thing Abraham did when he heard God's promise was to laugh (see Genesis 17:17). His was the laugh of faith. He said, in effect, "God, I know You can bring this to pass. I know You are a supernatural God."

And so often when God puts a promise in our hearts, it looks impossible. Maybe you're sick and God has assured you that you'll be healthy again. Or maybe you are struggling financially, but God is saying you're coming into overflow. He will prosper you. Perhaps your family is pulled apart. God promises to heal the bonds.

Your mind may have doubts. But remember to laugh in faith like Abraham, because it's just a matter of time before those promises come to pass. You are in a fixed fight.

I'm asking you today to get in the habit of taking your medicine on a regular basis. Every day, find some reason to laugh. Look for opportunities. If you don't think you have a reason, then just know you can laugh by faith. Keep a happy heart and a cheerful mind, and you will enjoy life more; even better, you will feel God's natural tranquilizers flow through you.

Today's Prayer

Father, I thank You for victory in every area of my life. Just as You laugh knowing the outcome, I choose to laugh by faith! I choose joy, I choose peace, and I choose to trust knowing my best days are right out in front of me. In Jesus' Name. Amen.

Today's Thought

When it gets tough and things don't look like they're going to work out, we know that with God we are on the winning team! Today you can laugh with Him, knowing that He has favor, strength, and victory in store for your future.

Smile and the World Smiles with You

Scripture Reading: Ephesians 4

Be kind and compassionate to one another, forgiving each other, just as in Christ God forgave you. EPHESIANS 4:32 NIV

I knew a steep charge was coming when I went to the airline counter to change the dates on four round-trip tickets. After I handed the tickets to the agent, she confirmed my fear.

"That's going to be fifty dollars extra per ticket," she said.

I laughed and smiled. "Yeah, I figured there would be a charge," I said.

My reaction seemed to surprise the ticket agent. "Why are you laughing?" she said. "Most people would be upset."

"I don't know," I replied. "I guess I'm just a happy person."

She shook her head and went to work on her computer. A few seconds later she handed me my new tickets and said, "I'm not going to charge you anything extra. We need more happy people around here."

The rest of that day I went around smiling and laughing at everybody who crossed my path!

My guess is that the airline ticket agent had dealt with all sorts of cranky and stressed-out people before I walked up to her counter. I wasn't happy about the thought of paying extra for changing my tickets, but I'd decided that the ticket agent didn't make the rules, so why should she have to deal with my unhappiness? I made the decision to treat her with good humor instead.

Is there always a payoff for wearing a smile instead of a frown? I think so. As I mentioned earlier, you'll enjoy better health with a positive approach to life, and also you will attract more friends, supporters, encouragers, and well-wishers.

Today's Prayer

Father, today I purpose in my heart to let the joy inside of me show up on my face. I choose to smile, to share life and kindness everywhere I go. Thank You for equipping me to be Your representative and sow seeds of life and victory everywhere I go. In Jesus' Name. Amen.

Today's Thought

We should always be on the lookout for ways we can be kind to one another. Can you share a smile with someone or an encouraging word? Can you help meet a need? Remember, as a believer, you are the hands and feet of Jesus on this earth. Look for ways to serve one another. Sow a seed and watch the harvest of blessing in your own life in return.

A Smile Brings Down the Walls

Scripture Reading: Psalm 126

Our mouths were filled with laughter, our tongues with songs of joy. Then it was said among the nations, "The LORD has done great things for them."
PSALM 126:2 NIV

Humor attracts people and bonds them to one another. That's one reason I start every sermon with a joke. It makes people more receptive. When I was growing up, my father's church held an annual Christmas banquet in the ballroom of a Houston hotel at the Galleria Mall. A thousand people attended those banquets.

Each year, the highlight of our Christmas banquet would be a fifteen-minute blooper film of funny things that had happened in church. We'd show clips of people sleeping and yawning through my dad's sermons. We might have other clips of kids acting up that we'd show in slow motion. Then we'd edit together various clips from my father's sermons, but we'd make him say funny things, or we'd speed him up and make him repeat the same phrase again and again so he sounded like a rap artist.

The audience would laugh for fifteen minutes nonstop. They'd still be laughing when the show ended and the lights came on. I'll never forget how all the serving crew from the hotel would come out to watch this video. The waiters, the cooks, and the busboys would line up along the walls around the ballroom to laugh with us.

Since the hotel was part of a mall, shoppers would hear the laughter, too. Within a few minutes, there would be a couple hundred people gathered at the doors, looking in and enjoying the fun.

Every now and then, I'd hear about a new member of the congregation who went shopping at the mall and found a place of worship with us, thanks to our ability to laugh and have fun while being strong in our faith. I guess it's no surprise that blooper shows and specials are so popular on television. Year after year, while other, more polished and more sophisticated shows fade away, people still watch the bloopers because they are so funny.

According to Psalm 126:2, when you're filled with laughter, others notice. It not only brings honor to God but your good example draws people to you.

Today's Prayer

Father, thank You for joy and laughter to lift my heart and the hearts of those around me. Help me bring honor to You by staying joyful and filled with faith. Let me always be the light that draws people to Your goodness. In Jesus' Name. Amen.

Today's Thought

Being willing to laugh at yourself and at life's ups and downs may be one of the greatest gifts you can have. We all know people who throw fits when they make mistakes. Some throw golf clubs. Others throw their bats and helmets. Those people are not fun to be around. But the person who is easygoing and laughs at mistakes is someone people love to spend time with.

Lock Into Laughter

Scripture Reading: Psalm 30

You turned my wailing into dancing: you removed my sackcloth and clothed me in joy.   PSALM 30:11 NIV

When we first moved into the former Compaq Center, the security folks gave me a key to the back area where we park our cars. This was a very strange-looking key. It was small and oblong, kind of fat, and plastic. I had never seen anything like it before. I went to try it on the door, but I could not figure out where to insert it. There was no slot for it. I tried to fit it in the doorknob key slot, thinking maybe it would open up more and take it. No luck.

After ten minutes of trying, I gave up and went to the security station and told the guard I couldn't figure out how to open the door.

He offered to go to the parking area and show me. So I gave him the key and back we went. When we arrived at the door, he reached up to the side of it and touched an electronic panel. I didn't even know it was up there!

When he just touched the panel, the door automatically opened because the "key" he'd given me put out an electronic signal to it, like a garage door opener or a remote car key.

When I told the guard how I'd tried to use the key in the doorknob, he laughed and laughed.

I thought, *I'm glad you think I am so funny, because you're going to miss working for me!*

You've heard the saying "If you can't beat them, join them." I ended up laughing more than him. Life is a lot more enjoyable when we don't take ourselves too seriously and we can laugh at our mistakes.

Today's Prayer

Father, thank You for the wonderful blessings You've given me in this life. Help me to be light-hearted and to have the boldness to laugh at myself and my mistakes rather than be embarrassed. Help me to keep my peace and joy as I learn, grow, and increase in You. In Jesus' Name. Amen.

Today's Thought

In tough times, it is easy to lose your joy. When you lose your joy, you lose your strength. When you don't have strength, you'll drag through the day defeated. When you're not strong, you'll catch diseases that you shouldn't have. Your immune system is run down. You're tired. You're worried. You're worn out. God says, "I've got a solution. In difficulties, cheer up. In famine, laugh. Keep your joy." I believe you can laugh your way to victory. You can laugh your way to better health. You can laugh your way to more energy.

Wrap Yourself in Humor

Scripture Reading: Matthew 25

I needed clothes and you clothed me.

MATTHEW 25:36 NIV

The other day I had breakfast alone in a hotel room, and afterward I wheeled the breakfast cart out into the hallway so it could be picked up. I forgot until the last moment that I only had my shorts on. Not gym shorts, underwear.

I'd already opened the door and had the cart halfway out when it hit me. I peeked my head out into the hall and nobody was out there, so I pushed the cart all the way out, but the back legs got stuck on the threshold.

I had to pick up the rear of the cart, lift it out of the room, step out into the hall, and push it against the wall.

As I did that, I heard a *click*.

That was the sound of my hotel room door closing and locking, with me in my underwear still out in the hallway.

My heart sank.

I saw a housekeeping cart about five doors down. I ran to it as fast as I could and got a towel and wrapped it around me. The cleaning lady came out, and I asked her if she could let me into my room.

"I need your ID for that," she said.

"I don't have my wallet, it's in the room," I answered.

She smiled and said, "You know, you look different on TV."

Then she kindly opened the door.

When unfortunate things happen, be secure enough in who you are to find the humor and laugh at yourself.

Today's Prayer

Father, thank You for covering me no matter what awkward situations I may face. Help me to always remember that humor has the power to heal embarrassment. Help me keep the right perspective and help me look for the opportunity to laugh each and every day. In Jesus' Name. Amen.

Today's Thought

When you find yourself in embarrassing situations sometimes the best way out is to find the humor and laugh.

Fill Your Home with Good Humor

Scripture Reading: Genesis 21

Sarah said, God has made me to laugh; all who hear will laugh with me.
GENESIS 21:6 AMP

I really appreciate that my wife loves to laugh. She keeps a fun atmosphere in our home. When Victoria laughs, she doesn't laugh to herself. She doesn't laugh under her breath. When she laughs, it fills the whole house with joy.

Her laugh is so contagious I can be sitting on the other side of the house, minding my own business, watching television, but when I hear her laughter, I feel like laughing, too. Before long I find myself laughing just because she's laughing.

If you have small children, there's no reason not to laugh every day, not just at them and their antics, but with them, too. Don't get so caught up in all the pressures of parenting that you don't take time to enjoy your children and see the humor in what they do.

When Jonathan was about two years old, I heard this loud screaming coming from his bedroom. I knew he was having a nightmare. I ran up there as fast as I could, opened the door, and there was Jonathan, sitting up in his bed, his eyes as big as saucers.

"Jonathan, what's wrong?"

"Daddy," he said, "the Holy Ghost is under my bed."

Our daughter, Alexandra, is equally entertaining. When she was about that same age, I'd work on my weekend messages for church in an office right outside our bedroom.

One day Alexandra strolled in and said, "Daddy, can we go play?"

"No, Alexandra, not right now. It'll be another hour or so before I finish this."

Every five minutes she returned.

"Daddy, is it time yet?"

Again and again, she'd ask me.

I felt a little frustrated with her so finally, when she showed up at my office door again, I said, "Alexandra, listen, I'm trying to concentrate. Please don't come back in. I'll come get you when I can play."

Five minutes later, the door creaks open and this sweet little-girl voice says, "Daddy, are you still trying to constipate?"

Today's Prayer

Father, thank You for Your joy, which is my strength. Help me to fill my home with laughter each and every day. Let my joy be contagious and draw others to your goodness. In Jesus' Name. Amen.

Today's Thought

Laughter is a great addition to every home. The enemy cannot stand the sound of you laughing. He cannot stand the sound of happy husbands and wives; family members having fun together. He wants there to be so much strife, tension, and pressure that we never have any joy in our homes. Don't fall into his trap. Keep your home filled with laughter and good humor each and every day.

Couples Who Laugh Together Stay Together

Scripture Reading: Proverbs 20

It is to one's honor to avoid strife, but every fool is quick to quarrel.

PROVERBS 20:3 NIV

Friends often ask Victoria and me about the secret to a healthy marriage. We always tell them two things: Number one, respect. Always be respectful, even when you disagree. And number two, laughter. Don't ever stop laughing together. Make sure your house is full of joy and happiness. We don't have to work at that; it seems to happen on its own.

The other day I walked into our bedroom and Victoria was over in the corner reading something with her back to me. I had come home much earlier than I had planned. I realized she hadn't heard me walk in. I debated whether to say something, but instead, I decided to just quietly wait for her to notice me. I thought that might be better than startling her.

When she turned around and I was there, she must have jumped three feet in the air. I know they say white people can't jump, but Victoria got some air.

She had this shocked look on her face, and I could not help but laugh and laugh.

The problem was that I tried to stop laughing, but the harder I tried, the funnier it hit me. After a minute or so of watching me laugh, Victoria finally gave in and began laughing, too.

By that time, I was over it.

But now she couldn't stop laughing.

It's easy to let the pressures of life weigh us down with stress and worry. I encourage you to keep laughter in your household. Remember, the couple that laughs together stays together.

Today's Prayer

Father, thank You for healthy, joy-filled relationships. Help me to always overlook offense and to daily stir up laughter. Give me opportunities to lighten the load of the people I love. Thank You for using me to share hope and love everywhere I go. In Jesus' Name. Amen.

Today's Thought

Remember the things you and your spouse enjoyed doing together, the fun and the laughter that made you always want to be together? Forget what's pulling you apart. Go back to the laughter that made you want to go from being single to being a couple.

Unleash Free-Flowing Laughter

Scripture Reading: Genesis 26

Isaac reopened the wells that had been dug in the time of his father Abraham, which the Philistines had stopped up after Abraham died, and he gave them the same names his father had given them.

GENESIS 26:18 NIV

In the Old Testament, enemies took over rival cities by clogging the wells that provided water to residents. They filled the wells with stones. This forced the people in the towns to leave the protection of the city walls in search of water. The enemy would then attack them.

You and I have wells of joy inside. As children, those wells flowed freely. We played and laughed and enjoyed each moment. But too often our wells become clogged as we grow older. Stones of disappointment, hurt, unforgiveness, stress, and doubt pile up and block the flow.

Genesis 26:18 says Isaac redug the wells that had been stopped up after his father, Abraham, died.

It's interesting, in part, because the name *Isaac* means "laughter." God is saying to unclog your wells with laughter so His goodness can once again live within.

When one of our sinks clogs up at home, I buy some Drano, pour it down the drain, and wait fifteen minutes. When I come back, the sink is unclogged. Laughter works like Drano. It cleans out whatever is clogging our lives. When you laugh regularly, it's just like you are cleaning out those pipes.

The instructions on the Drano bottle say to use it on a regular basis to keep the pipes free and clear. The same holds true with laughter. Pour it in, whenever you can. Find the humor in everyday moments. Make laughter a part of your everyday life. When you do that you will live healthier and you will enjoy your life more.

Today's Prayer

Father, today I choose to unclog the wells of joy! I choose to be happy. I choose to smile. I choose to laugh! Help me to make laughter a regular part of my days so I can live healthier and enjoy life more. In Jesus' Name. Amen.

Today's Thought

Laughter will help your relationships, too. Welcome it into your home. Make room for it. Clean out the spare bedroom if you have to. Open the doors and windows and let it fill your house.

PART
VI

Be a Dream Releaser

After You Climb High, Reach Back

Scripture Reading: Matthew 7

In everything, do to others what you would have them do to you, for this sums up the Law and the Prophets.　　MATTHEW 7:12 NIV

Michael is a talented musician who plays guitar for our services at Lakewood Church. He has performed with great musicians from around the world. He is at the top of his game, yet he is generous with his time and shares his talents with others. I know this well because Michael took our son, Jonathan, under his wing when Jonathan expressed an interest in playing the guitar.

We never asked Michael to teach Jonathan, and he has never requested payment, even though they've been working together more than eight years now. It's obvious Michael is a great teacher, because he's helped Jonathan become a great guitar player.

There is something more to know about Michael and his willingness to help others. Before he came to Lakewood, Michael led a different lifestyle than the one he leads today. He used drugs and partied. That lifestyle led to challenges, but Michael no longer uses drugs. He's not out partying on Friday nights anymore.

Now he is leading worship in our Celebrate Recovery classes. Michael has won, and now he is helping other people get free from addictions.

Our son, Jonathan, will always remember that Michael helped him develop his gifts as a great guitar player. Seventy years from now, he will still remember, *I'm successful in part because of Michael. He helped me to win. He brought the best out in me.* When you help someone win, you become a friend for life. You will always have a special place in their heart.

Today's Prayer

Father, thank You for the gifts, talents, and abilities You have given me. Help me to find ways to share these gifts with others. Show me ways to mentor and invest in the lives around me so they can rise up higher and be all that You've called them to be. In Jesus' Name. Amen.

Today's Thought

When you do for others what they cannot do for themselves, you will never lack God's favor. You will never lack God's blessing.

Be a Dream Releaser

Scripture Reading: Romans 12

Be devoted to one another in love.

ROMANS 12:10 NIV

Even as you work to accomplish your goals and build your own happy life, be sure to use your talent, your influence, and your experience to help those around you in need of a lift. There is nothing more rewarding than to end a day with the knowledge that you've helped someone else move closer to a dream.

You may have fulfilled your own goals for the day, but even better, you also took time to invest in someone else. It may have been just a two-minute phone call to encourage a friend or a younger person, or five minutes after work to help a coworker, or lending a hand to help a child with a school project.

When I look back over my life, outside of my family, I can think of four or five dream releasers—people who took special interest in me. A coach in high school spoke faith into me. I was the smallest on the team, but somehow he convinced me that I was the biggest, baddest, toughest player since Michael Jordan.

Another dream releaser, my Sunday school teacher Larry, invested in me. Larry, who still attends Lakewood Church, taught me and the other boys as if we were paying attention! He made it fun. He didn't just go by the lesson. He always went the extra mile. I can say now, "I'm successful in part because Larry helped me win."

You may not see my coach or Larry or my other dream releasers up here on the platform, but let me tell you, they are up here with me. I'm happy and successful because so many people reached back to me. They knew the value of helping someone else succeed and find joy.

Being successful doesn't necessarily make you great. What makes you great is when you reach back and help somebody else become great. Greatness is saying, "God has blessed me not to just sit on my throne and let everybody see my accomplishments. No, I know God has blessed me to become a blessing. God has helped me win so I can help someone else win."

Greatness comes to those who say, "God helped me overcome this addiction; now I'm going to go find somebody who's addicted and help them overcome." "God has blessed me with a happy, healthy family. I'm going to go find a family that's struggling and help them get back on track." Or, "God has helped me pass this course in high school. Now I'm going to go to my friend and help him study so he can pass, too."

Today's Prayer

Father, thank You for equipping me to be a blessing to others. Show me ways to be a dream releaser and help others to rise up higher. Help me use my influence to encourage others and honor You always. In Jesus' Name. Amen.

Today's Thought

There is nothing more rewarding than to lie down at night knowing that you helped someone else become better. Take time every day to invest, encourage, and inspire others. When you live as a dream releaser, you'll see your own dreams come to pass.

Help Others Win

Scripture Reading: Hebrews 13

Do not neglect to do good and to share what you have, for such sacrifices are pleasing to God. HEBREWS 13:16 ESV

In 1936 the Olympic Games were held in Berlin, Germany. Hitler was in control, and he didn't want any blacks to compete, much less win. One Nazi leader called blacks "non-humans." There was a young black American athlete by the name of Jesse Owens in the competition. Despite Hitler's wishes, Jesse already had won three gold medals, and he was about to compete for his fourth.

This event was the broad jump, now known as the running long jump. Jesse felt hostility from the haters in the crowd, and he began to lose focus. On his first attempt he faulted. The judges claimed he crossed the line before he jumped. He was faulted again on his second attempt.

One more fault and he would be disqualified. This was very much out of character for Jesse, but he'd let the crowd's boos and name-calling get to him. They were still jeering at him and shouting against him. He was very rattled.

Jesse's main competitor was a tall German athlete named Luz Long. They did not know each other. Jesse may have assumed that Luz Long, who was a sports hero in his country, was his enemy, too.

But in front of tens of thousands of people, Luz Long did what seemed unthinkable in that setting. He walked up, put his arm around Jesse Owens, and offered some advice.

He said, "Jesse, the qualifying distance is only twenty-three feet. You've jumped twenty-six feet many times before. Just move your starting mark back three inches, and that way you'll make sure to jump before the line so they can't disqualify you."

Jesse took his advice, and on the next jump he qualified. The black American went on to break the world record and win his fourth gold medal. He beat out Luz Long on his final jump, but Long was the first to congratulate him.

Jesse Owens later said of his German dream releaser, "It took a lot of courage for him to befriend me in front of Hitler. You can melt all the medals and cups I have, and they wouldn't be a plating on the 24-karat friendship I felt for Luz Long at that moment."

I've found the greatest legacy is not what we leave *for* people, but what we leave *in* people. Luz Long, who died during World War II, left Jesse Owens with a memory of courage and friendship that he never forgot— and neither did the rest of the world.

Today's Prayer

Father, by faith I ask for the opportunity to fulfill someone's dream today. Give me creative ideas that will show Your love and help others win at life. Give me Your heart of compassion, let Your grace flow through me as I encourage others to succeed. In Jesus' Name. Amen.

Today's Thought

I've heard it said, "No one stands taller on their climb for success than when he bends down to help somebody else." If you will live unselfishly and be willing to give advice like Luz Long, you will always have God's blessings. When you are a dream releaser, God will make sure your dreams come to pass.

Give the Gift of a Dream

Scripture Reading: Philippians 2

Let each of you look not only to his own interests, but also to the interests of others.　　　　　　　　　　　　　　　Philippians 2:4 esv

Shay was ten years old and both physically and mentally challenged, but he loved baseball. One day he and his father walked by a baseball field where a bunch of young boys Shay's age were playing a game.

"Do you think they would let me play on one of their teams?" Shay asked his father.

Shay's dad knew that he couldn't play at the same level as the other boys, but he didn't want to disappoint his son. The father asked one of the boys in the dugout if Shay could play. The little boy looked around at his friends, trying to get some advice. Finally he said, "Well, sir. There are only two innings left and we're down by three runs. Sure, he can come play. We'll put him in the outfield."

Shay was so excited. He took the field with joy, just radiating happiness. In the last inning their team was down by one run. There were two outs, with a runner on third, and it was Shay's turn to bat.

His teammates considered using a pinch hitter in hopes of winning the game, but they decided it wouldn't be right to take Shay out. They sent him to the plate with little hope that he could hit the ball. They thought they'd already lost the game. The other team had a very good pitcher.

The star pitcher wound up and threw the first pitch so fast, Shay didn't see it coming. He swung late and missed it by a mile. At that point the pitcher realized that Shay had some physical challenges. The next pitch he threw at about half the speed of the first. But once again Shay swung and missed.

This time the pitcher stepped off the mound and walked closer to home plate. He threw the ball as softly as he could, and believe it or not, Shay hit it. The ball dribbled about five feet and stopped in front of the pitcher's mound. The pitcher ran and picked it up.

Just out of instinct he was about to fire it to first base and win the game, but out of the corner of his eye he saw Shay struggling to run the best he could. The pitcher's heart took over for his instincts. He threw the ball over the first baseman's head into the outfield.

Shay's dad yelled, "Run, Shay! Run!"

The runner on third scored while Shay rounded first and headed toward second. By this time all the other boys knew what was going on. The outfielder threw the ball over the shortstop's head. The player backing up the shortstop let it go through his legs.

Shay rounded third base and the whole crowd was cheering his name. He scored the winning run while his father watched in tears. Shay was nearly bursting with joy when he crossed the plate and was hugged by his teammates.

Shay's team won the game, but all of those boys won God's favor that day. Sometimes you have to give up winning one thing to win something even bigger. In this case, those boys on the opposing team won a friend for life. They gave something to Shay that he will never forget.

Sometimes you have to make sacrifices to let someone else step ahead. Sometimes you have to put your own dreams on hold temporarily so you can help release a dream in somebody else.

What you make happen for others, God will make happen for you. When you live unselfishly and you help somebody else get ahead, God will make sure someone is there to help you get ahead.

My challenge to you is to make every day a Shay day. Find somebody to invest in, a person you can help come up higher. Don't go to bed without knowing you did something for someone to help them win. Believe in people before they succeed. Call out those seeds of greatness.

Today's Prayer

Father, by faith I ask for the opportunity to fulfill someone's dream today. Give me creative ideas that will show Your love and help others win at life. Give me Your heart of compassion, let Your grace flow through me as I encourage others to succeed. In Jesus' Name. Amen.

Today's Thought

When you do for others what they cannot do for themselves, you will always have God's favor. You will accomplish your dreams, and then God will take you higher and higher.

Draw Out the Best in Others

Scripture Reading: 2 Corinthians

We are therefore Christ's ambassadors, as though God were making his appeal through us.   2 CORINTHIANS 5:20 NIV

A young man who'd been struggling with finding direction in his life was home for a visit from college in 1975. He visited his mother's beauty shop and found a regular customer, Ruth Green, was having her hair done. He greeted her and sat down, but grew nervous because she was staring so intently at him.

Finally Ms. Green lifted the hairdryer off her head and said, "Somebody get me a pen and a piece of paper."

She wrote down a vision she'd had about the young man when he walked into his mother's shop. She handed it to him and it said: "You will speak to millions. You will travel the world and you will make a positive difference."

The young man put that prophecy in his wallet and in his heart. In the years that followed, whenever he became discouraged in his acting career, he pulled out Ms. Green's prophecy. It reminded him that someone believed in him.

To this day, Denzel Washington, the Academy Award–winning actor, carries around that prophecy. Who knows where he would be if Ms. Green hadn't taken the time to bless his future. Who knows if he would have been such a success if she hadn't planted those seeds of faith in his heart. You never know the impact a small note, a kind word of encouragement, can have.

We can either draw out the best in people or we can draw out the worst. I read that 75 percent of people in prison reported that either their parents or their guardians had predicted in childhood where they would end up. The wrong seeds were planted. Low expectations were set.

When a child is told to expect the worst, the child becomes the worst. I often wonder what would have happened if somebody had told some of the people in our nation's prisons that they might one day be doctors or entrepreneurs or great teachers. There's no telling where those inmates might have ended up if only they'd had people builders in their lives.

If only someone had believed in them and taken the time to draw out their gifts, to listen to their dreams, to see what they were good at, and then encourage them to be the best they could be. If only someone had given them permission to succeed instead of a prediction that they would fail.

Today's Prayer

Father, use me to speak life and blessing over the people around me. Give me opportunities to draw out the dreams in others' hearts. Give me boldness to share the Good News and lead people down Your path of blessing and victory. In Jesus' Name. Amen.

Today's Thought

Make it your mission today to speak faith and victory into people. Call out their seeds of greatness and help them become who God created them to be.

Cast Your Votes of Confidence

Scripture Reading: 1 Thessalonians

Encourage one another and build each other up, just as in fact you are doing. 1 Thessalonians 5:11 NIV

Reggie Jackson, the Hall of Fame baseball player, said, "A great manager has the ability to make a player think that he is better than he is. He convinces you to have confidence in yourself. He lets you know that he believes in you, and before long you discover talent that you never knew you had."

That's what happens when we believe the best about someone. We draw out the best. In the Scripture quoted above, the word *encourage* simply means "to urge forward." Every one of us should have someone we believe in, someone we're urging forward, someone we're helping to achieve goals and dreams.

How do you encourage someone? You study that person and identify what he or she does well. What excites him? What are her strengths? An encourager sees things in others that they often can't see in themselves. A simple compliment, a single word of encouragement, can give a person the confidence he or she needs to take that step of faith.

Even Henry Ford benefited from encouragement in his early days, and one of his boosters was none other than Thomas Edison. The pioneering automaker was introduced to Edison as "the man trying to build a car that ran on gasoline." When Edison heard this, his face lit up. He slammed his fist on the table and said, "You've got it. A car that has its own power plant; that's a brilliant idea."

Up to that point, Henry Ford had dealt with many naysayers and discouragers. He had just about convinced himself to give up, but along came Edison and spoke faith into him. That was a turning point in Henry Ford's life.

"I thought I had a good idea, but I started to doubt myself," he once said. "Then came along one of the greatest minds that's ever lived and gave me his complete approval."

A simple vote of confidence helped launched the automotive industry. We don't realize the power we hold. We don't always realize what it means when we tell somebody, "I believe in you. You've got what it takes. I'm behind you 100 percent."

Cast your vote. Step up and volunteer to be someone's number one fan. Encourage them. Lift them up when they are down. Celebrate when they succeed. Pray when they are struggling. Urge them to keep pressing forward. That's what it means to be a people builder.

Today's Prayer

Father, help me to believe the best about others. Help me to always use my words to encourage and speak life. Thank You for choosing me and using me to be a miracle to others and bring glory to You. In Jesus' Name. Amen.

Today's Thought

Every day, we have opportunities to show God's love and compassion to others by meeting their needs and offering them hope and encouragement. I encourage you today to look for ways to be a blessing to someone else. When you pour into others and help meet their needs, God will make sure that others pour into you.

Kind Words Can Change Lives

Scripture Reading: Proverbs 12

The words of the reckless pierce like swords, but the tongue of the wise brings healing.   PROVERBS 12:18 NIV

A teenage girl struggled with anorexia. She stood nearly six feet tall but weighed less than one hundred pounds. She wouldn't eat but a couple hundred calories a day. She became depressed and disillusioned. She cut off ties to friends and family. Starvation seemed like a reasonable option to her because she felt she had no purpose.

One day a longtime friend from school called and asked if she would help her with math homework. She pleaded for help, so the anorexic teen agreed to help her. They worked together on the problems and afterward the friend said, just in passing, "You are so smart and you have such a way of explaining things. You would make a great math teacher one day."

That simple comment planted a seed within this troubled teen. The encouraging words gave her a sense of purpose. She realized that she had talent, and that she had something to give others. Her perspective changed, and so did the course of her life.

Twenty years later, she is a healthy and happy mother of three and an award-winning math teacher who works with underachieving children. She credits the turnaround in her life to the words of the girl she'd helped with her math homework.

A simple affirmation, an encouraging comment, or a bit of praise can make a huge difference. When you bless people with your words, you speak faith into them. One thing you can be certain of is that people never grow tired of hearing compliments and encouragements. You can go on and on about how wonderful they are and they'll never be bored! That's proof of just how much we hunger for praise and direction in our lives.

Mark Twain said, "I can live for a whole year off of one good compliment." Whom can you give the gift of encouragement to? Don't leave out even those who seem to have accomplished more than most. Everyone wants to be appreciated.

You have the power to help someone go to a higher level. The people in your life are not there by accident. Are you believing in them? Are you urging them forward? Are you speaking the blessing?

When you bring out the best in others, the best will be brought out in you. Remember, an encouraging word works wonders. Be free with your compliments. Tell people what they mean to you. Get in the habit of building up those around you. When you sow those seeds, God will make sure you go higher, too.

Today's Prayer

Father, help me to always bring out the best in others. Help me to bless people with my words, to give the gift of encouragement, and to always speak words of life. Thank You for filling my heart with affirmation so that I can affirm those around me today and every day. In Jesus' Name. Amen.

Today's Thought

Find at least one person you can build up. You may find four or five different people. Write their names on a sheet of paper. List what you like about them, their strengths. Pray over that. Ask God to show you ways to bless them. And then speak favor into their lives. Write them encouraging notes. Let them know you believe in them. As they succeed, so will you.

Give Up Your Comfort to Comfort Others

Scripture Reading: Luke 10

[Jesus asked,] "Which of these three do you think was a neighbor to the man who fell into the hands of robbers?" The expert in the law replied, "The one who had mercy on him." Jesus told him, "Go and do likewise."
Luke 10:36–37 niv

Jesus told about the good Samaritan who was riding his donkey and saw a man who had been beaten and left for dead on the roadside. He lifted the injured man onto his donkey and took him to a place where he could recover. I love the fact that the good Samaritan let the injured man ride while he walked because sometimes, to comfort others, you may have to give up your own comfort. Sometimes you have to trade places with those who are hurting.

To be a healer, you have to be willing to be inconvenienced. You might have to miss dinner in order to wipe away a tear. You might have to skip a workout to help a couple work through their challenges. You may even have to drive across town and pick up that coworker struggling with an addiction and then bring him to church.

A true healer doesn't mind inconvenience, or taking risks in the course of reaching out to those who truly need a hand up. Jim Bakker, the fallen minister and cohost of *The PTL Club* television show, went to prison for five years on fraud convictions. When he was about to be released, Franklin Graham, Billy Graham's son, contacted him and said his family had rented him a house and provided a car for him.

"Franklin, you can't do that," Bakker told him. "I have too much baggage. You'll be criticized. Your ministry can't be associated with me."

Franklin said, "Sure we can, Jim. You were our friend before, and you will be our friend afterward."

The first Sunday after his release, Jim Bakker was living temporarily in a halfway house as a condition of the court. Ruth Graham, Billy Graham's wife, called the place and asked the man in charge if Jim could have permission to leave and come to church with the Grahams that Sunday. The judge agreed. When Jim entered the church, they ushered him right down to the very front row and sat him next to Franklin Graham.

The Grahams had ten or fifteen family members there. There were two vacant seats next to Jim Bakker before the service started. He didn't know who they were for. But when the music kicked up, a side door opened and out walked Billy and Ruth Graham. They sat right next to Jim Bakker. He had been out of prison only forty-eight hours, but the whole world was put on notice that the Grahams still considered Jim Bakker a friend.

What were the Grahams doing associating with a convicted criminal? They were loving him back into wholeness. They were acting as healers.

Today's Prayer

Father, help me respond to those in need the way the good Samaritan did. Help me always find time to show mercy and love. Use me to bring healing and restoration to the hurting. In Jesus' Name. Amen.

Today's Thought

I heard someone say, "A true friend walks in when everybody else walks out. A true friend doesn't rub it in when you make a mistake. They help rub it out." That's a question to ask yourself when someone you know falls off the path. Are you rubbing it in or rubbing it out? Are you a healer and a restorer, or are you critical and judgmental?

Healing God's Children

Scripture Reading: Psalm 145

The Lord *is merciful and compassionate, slow to get angry and filled
with unfailing love. The* Lord *is good to everyone. He showers compassion on all his creation.*   Psalm 145:8–9 nlt

Singer Tammy Trent went to Jamaica with her husband, Trent Lender-
ink, shortly after their eleventh wedding anniversary. They rock-climbed
and went to the beach for several days and then, just before they were supposed to leave, Trent decided to check out the blue lagoon, a favorite diving spot on the island. Trent was an avid scuba diver, but he didn't have his
gear this time. Instead, he dove into the lagoon with just fins and a snorkel
while Tammy watched. She didn't worry because Trent often dove like
this. He could stay underwater for up to ten minutes free diving.

Ten minutes or so went by and Tammy began looking for her husband.
He had not yet come up for air, and she grew worried. Fifteen minutes—
still nothing; twenty minutes…panic set in. Tammy called the authori-
ties. Tragically, Trent had drowned. They recovered his body the next day.

Tammy, who had been with Trent since high school, was in shock, totally
devastated, and she was alone in this foreign country. She called her parents
and they said they would come immediately. The first available flight was
the next morning, which just happened to be September 11, 2001, the day

the terrorists struck in the United States. All flights were grounded. Tammy's parents could not go to her, and she could not leave Jamaica.

Tammy was so distraught. She prayed, "God, if You're up there anywhere, please send somebody to help me, somebody to let me know that You care."

A little later there was a knock on her hotel door room. It was the housekeeper. She was an older Jamaican woman. She said, "I was cleaning the room next door. I don't mean to bother you, but I couldn't help but hear you crying, and I was wondering if there is anything that I could pray with you about."

Tammy told her what had happened. That older Jamaican woman put her loving arms around Tammy and held her like she was her very own daughter. That moment, thousands of miles from home, Tammy Trent knew that God was still in control.

The Jamaican housekeeper was living as a healer. She was sensitive to the needs of those around her. She heard the cries for help coming from another room. She could have thought, *Oh, I've got a lot of work to do. I'm busy. I've got problems of my own.* Instead, she dropped what she was doing and embraced one of God's children. She knew her assignment in life was to help wipe away the tears. That moment, she poured the healing oil onto Tammy's wounds.

She simply let her know that she cared. She was the first step in Tammy's long period of healing.

Today's Prayer

Father, today and every day I make myself available to You. Let me be Your hands of healing in the earth. Let me wipe the tears of others and lift their spirits, always pointing the way to You. In Jesus' Name. Amen.

Today's Thought

The Scripture says, "Jesus was a friend of sinners." When you show mercy to the guilty, when you encourage the discouraged, when you lift people up as everyone else is pushing them down, you touch the heart of God in a very special way.

Follow the Flow of Compassion

Scripture Reading: Revelation 21

*He will wipe every tear from their eyes, and there will be no more death
or sorrow or crying or pain. All these things are gone forever.*

REVELATION 21:4 NLT

Victoria called a friend named Shannon a while back. A young lady
answered and seemed somewhat troubled. Victoria said, "Shannon, is
this you?"

The voice was muffled and said, "Yes, this is me and I'm going to be
okay."

Confused, Victoria gave Shannon's full name and asked again if she
had the right number. The young lady said, "No, you must have the wrong
number. This is a different Shannon."

Victoria was about to hang up, but she felt this flow of compassion
toward the person on the line.

"Shannon, I know this may sound strange, but can I pray with you
about something?" she asked.

The woman began to weep.

"Would you please? My father just died, and I'm so depressed I don't
know what I'm going to do."

Victoria prayed and spoke faith to her. She comforted her as best she
could, assuring her that God was at her side. Before she hung up, the

young lady said, "You're my angel. Now I know that God still has a plan for my life."

God will bring people across our paths so we can restore them. Be sensitive and follow that flow of compassion.

Today's Prayer

Father, help me be sensitive to Your flow of compassion. I choose to respond to the prompting in my heart to love and minister to others. Use me today for Your glory to help those in need of a touch from You. In Jesus' Name. Amen.

Today's Thought

The Scripture says that one day God will wipe away all the tears. There will be no more tragedy, no more sickness, and no more pain. But in the meantime, God is counting on you and me to wipe away these tears. You can sense when someone is hurting. All of a sudden, you feel a flow of compassion and you think, *I need to go pray for them. I need to go encourage them.* Don't ignore those instincts. That's God wanting you to bring healing.

Take the Time to Care

Scripture Reading: Proverbs 4

My child, pay attention to what I say. Listen carefully to my words. Don't lose sight of them. Let them penetrate deep into your heart, for they bring life to those who find them, and healing to their whole body.
PROVERBS 4:20–22 NLT

I was at the hospital visiting with a friend when a mother and daughter recognized me in the hallway. They asked if I would go down the hall and pray for the woman's husband, the father of the young woman.

When I arrived at his room, they said they would wait outside. I thought that was a little strange, but I went. The man was about sixty years old. I did not know him, but we visited for ten or fifteen minutes. Then I prayed over him. I gave him a big hug.

When I walked out, the mother and daughter were grinning from ear to ear.

"What is so funny?" I asked them.

"We can't believe he let you pray for him," the mother said. "He doesn't even like you."

I thought, *Oh, thanks a lot. That's why I went in by myself.*

"When we watch you on television, he always makes fun of you and tells us to turn you off," she added.

I thought: *If I had known that, I might have prayed a little bit differently.*

But when you take time to care, you never know what God will do. That was years ago, and today do you know that man and his family come to services at Lakewood every week? They never miss a Sunday!

Come to find out, that man used to be a deacon in another church, but he'd been mistreated and hadn't gone to any church in thirty years!

Today's Prayer

Father, help me show unconditional love everywhere I go. Use me to heal, encourage, and inspire the people You bring across my path. Help me be sensitive to Your leading, to reach out and sow seeds of life to others. In Jesus' Name. Amen.

Today's Thought

When you live as a healer, you break down the walls. You soften hard hearts. Love never fails.

Healing Faith

Scripture Reading: Luke 15

Jesus told them this parable: "Suppose one of you has a hundred sheep and loses one of them. Doesn't he leave the ninety-nine in the open country and go after the lost sheep until he finds it? And when he finds it, he joyfully puts it on his shoulders and goes home. Then he calls his friends and neighbors together and says, 'Rejoice with me; I have found my lost sheep.' I tell you that in the same way there will be more rejoicing in heaven over one sinner who repents than over ninety-nine righteous persons who do not need to repent." LUKE 15:3–7 NIV

Years ago, my father went to a service across town at a friend's church. He arrived late, so he sat in the back row. After a few minutes, a young man walked in looking very troubled. My father felt that flow of compassion and made a note to reach out to him after the service.

But midway through, the young man walked out. My father felt so strongly he went after him. He looked in the lobby and couldn't find him. He went out into the parking lot, searched and searched. Still nothing. He came back in and checked the restroom, and sure enough, there he was.

My father looked the young man in the eyes and said, "I don't know you, but I want to tell you God's hand is on your life. He's got a destiny for you to fulfill. Don't give up on your future."

The young man wept.

"My life is so messed up," he said. "I'm addicted to so many drugs. I decided to come to church one more time, and then I was going to go home and take every pill I could find."

Later, this young man recalled that when he walked into the church, one of the first things he noticed was my father's shoes. Then, when he'd walked out, he'd seen my father following him, and "Everywhere I went, I saw those shoes following me."

My father wore the shoes of a healer. The shoes of a restorer. The shoes of a minister tracking down prodigals and healing hearts.

That night was a turning point in the young man's life. Today, more than thirty years later, he's the pastor of a very successful church. But I wonder where he would be if my father had not been living as a healer?

A hundred years from now if someone were to remember me, I don't want them to say, "Oh, yeah. Joel, he's the guy that had a big church. He wrote some nice books. He was kind of popular."

No, I want them to say, "That man was a healer. He was a restorer. He lifted the fallen. He encouraged the discouraged. He gave mercy to the guilty. He spent his life wiping away the tears."

I received a letter just recently from a lady who said that for more than forty years she'd felt beaten down by life and abandoned by her religion. She was told that God loved her only when she kept all the rules and followed all the man-made laws.

"I suffered under religion," she said. "I could never be good enough."

She ended up dropping out of church depressed and confused. Twelve years later she was flipping through the channels, and she heard me talking about God's unconditional love and how God has a great plan for all of us.

For the first time, she felt a freedom on the inside, she said. It was like God had breathed new life into her spirit.

"Joel, sometimes, because you don't condemn people, others criticize you and say you're just preaching 'Christianity lite,'" she said. "But let me tell you, I lived under 'Christianity heavy' for forty-two years. I was broken. I was defeated. I was depressed. But today I am healthy. I'm happy. I'm whole. I'm helping others.

"I will take 'Christianity lite' over 'Christianity heavy' any day of the week," she said.

Religion likes to beat people down. Religion will criticize you because you're not hard enough on others. But I love what Jesus said: "My yoke is easy and My burden is light" (Matthew 11:30 NKJV).

I don't see the need to beat anyone down. Life does that enough to people. I encourage you to be a healer and a restorer of dreams. Look for those you can lift up instead. Help them reclaim their happiness and joy. You are a container filled with God. Release His healing wherever you go, and I can assure you, God's face will always shine down upon you.

Today's Prayer

Father, help me to always wear the shoes of a healer. Help me to wear the shoes of a restorer. I choose to be the one to go after the lost and hurting and lonely and bring them back to You. Thank You for filling me with Your love and compassion as I fulfill Your mission in the earth. In Jesus' Name. Amen.

Today's Thought

The book of James talks about how we need to go after the prodigals. We need to go after those who have fallen away. If you know of people who were once strong in faith but have weakened, go after them. They need healing, too. They need their happiness and joy restored. Your attitude should be: *I'm on a mission from God. If you fall away, you're on dangerous ground, because I will track you down. I'm going to help bring you back into the fold.*

PART
VII

Celebrate Yourself

Encourage Yourself

Scripture Reading: 1 Samuel 30

*And David was greatly distressed; for the people spake of stoning him,
because the soul of all the people was grieved, every man for his sons and
for his daughters: but David encouraged himself in the* LORD *his God.*

1 SAMUEL 30:6 NKJV

One of the battles we all have to fight is the battle with discouragement. Our dreams don't always come true on our timetables. We go
through disappointments and adversities. It's easy to lose enthusiasm, happiness, and joy and zeal for life. In those times, it's good to have family and
friends who encourage us. It's good to have a coach, a teacher, or a pastor
to cheer us on.

But one thing I've learned is that other people cannot keep us encouraged. Other people cannot keep us cheered up. They may give us a boost.
They may help us from time to time. But if we really want to live in victory, that encouragement has to come from the inside. We must learn to
encourage ourselves.

This is especially true when times get tough and things aren't going
your way. At those moments, you may not feel like pursuing your dreams.
Your mind may be telling you, *It's not worth it. It's never going to get any
better. You might as well just settle where you are.* Deep down in your spirit
there has to be a resolve, a strength on the inside that says, *I refuse to settle*

where I am. I know God has a great plan for my life, and I'm going to keep pressing forward and become everything that He's created me to be.

This is what King David had to do, according to Scripture. He had just suffered a major setback. It was one of the most difficult times of his life. His city had been destroyed. His family had been kidnapped. And now his own men had turned against him. The situation looked impossible. He could have easily just given up and faded off into the sunset defeated and depressed. But the Scripture says, "David strengthened himself in the LORD his God" (1 Samuel 30:6 NKJV).

David understood this principle. He wasn't depending on his family, his friends, or his colleagues. This is one of the secrets to David's success. He knew how to draw encouragement and strength from the inside. How did he do it? He began to replay the victories God had given him in the past. He remembered how God chose him from the other brothers when he was a shepherd boy. He remembered how he killed the lion and the bear with his bare hands. He remembered how God helped him defeat Goliath and how God protected him when King Saul was trying to kill him.

As David rehearsed over and over in his mind the goodness and faithfulness of God, strength began to fill his heart. He created a new vision of victory. He thanked God for what He had done. He thanked God that He could turn the situation around. David went from being depressed and defeated to rising up with a warrior mentality.

Today's Prayer

Father, teach me to encourage myself the way David encouraged himself. Help me create a vision of victory by rehearsing your goodness and faithfulness in my mind. Help me always see that You are my strength and hope, and through You all things are possible. In Jesus' Name. Amen.

Today's Thought

Sometimes when you need encouragement the most, those you're counting on to cheer you up won't be there, unfortunately. The friend who normally calls may be out of town. Your spouse may be having a tough month. Your coworkers or your parents may be preoccupied with their own challenges. But when you learn to dig down deep and encourage yourself, there is a real freedom.

Every Setback Is a Setup for a Comeback

Scripture Reading: 1 Samuel 30

David recovered everything the Amalekites had taken, including his two wives. Nothing was missing: young or old, boy or girl, plunder or anything else they had taken. David brought everything back. He took all the flocks and herds, and his men drove them ahead of the other livestock, saying, "This is David's plunder." 1 SAMUEL 30:18–20 NIV

I see too many people today who have just settled where they are. Giving in to the spirit of discouragement steals our dreams. The attitude of those who settle for less is: *It's not worth it. My marriage is not worth fighting for. It's never going to work out.* Or, *I'm tired of dealing with this child. It's not worth the struggle. I'm tired of doing what's right; I'm never going to get ahead.* No, don't believe those lies. That is the spirit of discouragement trying to steal your dreams and keep you right where you are.

Don't you dare settle where you are. You may have suffered a setback. Like David in the Bible, you've been through a disappointment. Maybe a relationship didn't work out. Maybe you're facing a major health issue right now. Remember this: Every setback is a setup for a comeback.

You may have been knocked down, but you weren't knocked out. You've got to get back up, dust yourself off. God has you in the palm of His hand. He said if you would stay in faith, He would not only bring you out, He would bring you out better off than you were before.

This is what David had to do. He was down, but he didn't stay down. He mentally replayed his victories. He thanked God for what He had done in the past. When he changed the channel and took on an attitude of faith and expectancy, David went from being a victim to being a victor. He said to his men, "Get up, guys. We're going to go attack the enemy."

The Scripture says they not only recovered everything that had been stolen from them, but they came out with more than they had before. That's what God wants to do for every one of us. But it all started when David encouraged himself. He recognized the main battle wasn't taking place on the outside. It was taking place on the inside.

When all the odds were against him—his family wasn't there, his friends had turned on him, the news wasn't good, the economy was low, gas was high—his attitude was, "I'm not worried about any of that. I know the God I serve is well able to deliver me."

David said, in effect, "I've seen God lift me out of the pit before. He set my feet on a rock, put a new song in my heart. And if He did it for me back then, I know He'll do it for me right now." That's the kind of attitude that gets God's attention.

Today's Prayer

Father, today I declare that with You, all things are possible! I thank You that You are turning every setback into a setup for a comeback. Thank You for placing my feet on solid rock and putting a new song of praise in my heart as I stand and see Your salvation in every area of my life. In Jesus' Name. Amen.

Today's Thought

Every promise God has put in your heart, every dream He's planted on the inside, is well worth the fight. Your child is worth it. Your marriage is worth it. Your health is worth it. Your dreams are worth it.

Celebrate Yourself

Scripture Reading: Psalm 100

Make a joyful noise unto the LORD, all ye lands. Serve the LORD with gladness: come before his presence with singing. Know ye that the LORD he is God: it is he that hath made us, and not we ourselves; we are his people, and the sheep of his pasture.   PSALM 100:1–3 KJV

A young lady named Brittany moved to a new school in junior high. Most of the students had grown up together and been friends for years and years. She was having a tough time breaking in and really connecting with anybody.

This school had a tradition that during the week before Valentine's Day, students could buy 25-cent carnations to send to one another. The carnations were all delivered during homeroom on Valentine's Day in front of the whole class. So it was a big deal to see how many carnations everyone received.

Well, Brittany knew she would not receive any carnations. She was new to the school and didn't have any friends. She was dreading that day, thinking she'd be left out and embarrassed.

But then Brittany came up with a great idea. Instead of just sitting back and watching everybody else get flowers, she decided to send some to herself. She took five dollars down to the school office, where she asked for twenty carnation delivery forms. Then she filled them out in private so nobody would know she was sending them to herself.

On Valentine's Day, most of the young ladies received three or four carnations. The real popular girls might have five or six or seven delivered to them. But in Brittany's homeroom, it seemed every other carnation came to her. Her homeroom classmates looked at her, thinking, *Who in the world is this girl? She has so many friends.*

One after another carnation was delivered to her. Her classmates would ask, "Who's that from?" And Brittany would look at the note and say, "Oh. They are so special. They love me so much. I can't wait to tell them thanks."

They had no idea she was talking about herself. You would have thought Brittany was the most popular girl in school. By the end of Valentine's Day, she was the envy of the whole class. She had more carnations than anybody else.

You need Brittany's attitude: *If nobody else is celebrating me right now, I'm going to celebrate myself. If nobody is asking me out to dinner, I'm going to dress up and take myself out to dinner. If nobody is sending me a birthday gift, watch out. I'm going to buy myself a present.*

Today's Prayer

Father, You said in Your word that we are to love others as we love ourselves. So today I'm choosing to love and celebrate myself because I am fearfully and wonderfully made. Help me love others out of the abundance of my heart. In Jesus' Name. Amen.

Today's Thought

It is easy to stay encouraged when you learn to compliment yourself. Sometimes we think it's humble to compliment somebody else while putting ourselves down. Instead, be confident and encouraging to yourself. Celebrate yourself to build strength within.

Tune Your Ears to the Positive

Scripture Reading: 1 Chronicles 22

Set your mind and heart to seek (inquire of and require as your vital necessity) the Lord your God.   1 CHRONICLES 22:19 AMP

We have two shih tzu dogs, Daisy and Spirit, who are amazing pets. Spirit has supersensitive hearing. She is so tuned in to her surroundings, she can hear people coming to the front door long before they get there. She'll start barking ten or fifteen seconds before they ring the doorbell. She has trained herself to hear what she wants to hear.

Spirit loves cheese, and she can hear when we're opening a bag of it, even if she's out in the yard. Spirit immediately comes running into the kitchen, sits at our feet, and waits for her piece of cheese.

When the whole family is in the kitchen, there are all kinds of noises, all kinds of sounds. Jonathan is pouring cereal. Alexandra is opening chips. I'm using the blender. Victoria is wrapping up food. Spirit sits as calm as can be; she never even flinches. But the moment anyone touches the cheese, she goes on alert.

Her attitude is: *It's my time now. I am ready for my snack.*

Why is that? She has trained herself to hear what's important to her. She doesn't care if I get the bread out. She doesn't care if I open the chips or unwrap the lettuce. Everything else goes in one ear and out the other. All she's concerned about is the cheese, and she is keenly aware of that sound.

What sound are you tuned in to? Some people have a habit of tuning in to the negative. They're drawn to it, almost like they feed off of it. If a thought comes that says, *It's going to be a lousy day*, they just take the bait. "Oh, yeah, it is going to be a lousy day."

Don't let that be you. You've got to retrain your ears. Tune out the negative and start listening for faith-filled thoughts. When you wake up after you ignore all the negative thoughts, eventually you're going to hear, "This is the day the Lord has made. This is going to be a great day."

If you trained yourself to hear the bad, you can train yourself to hear the good. Next time a negative thought comes, just say, "No thanks, that's not for me."

Let the negative thoughts bounce off you like water off a duck's back. Just like Spirit sat there unfazed by the sound of the chips and the cereal and the bread, dismiss those thoughts that are not productive and positive. Eventually you will hear the right sound. Something will open up positive thoughts, such as *I'm talented*. It will be just like an alarm going off in your spirit. Rise up and say, "Yes, I'll take that one. I am talented," or "Yes, that's for me. I am well able. I am more than a conqueror."

Today's Prayer

Father, today I choose to tune in to You. Your Word says that I am Your sheep, I hear Your voice, and the voice of a stranger I will not follow. Help me to tune out negative voices and negative, self-defeating thoughts so I can clearly receive Your truth today. In Jesus' Name. Amen.

Today's Thought

It's amazing how we can train our ears to hear what we want to hear. Train yourself to latch on to positive, hopeful thoughts. Be disciplined in your thoughts so that you can weed out discouraging, negative thoughts. Don't give them the time of day.

Detox Your Mind

Scripture Reading: Proverbs 4

Above all else, guard your heart, for everything you do flows from it.
PROVERBS 4:23 NIV

We hear a lot about detoxing our bodies and how there are chemicals in our food that can be harmful, certain hormones and bacteria that can build up, even pesticides in the air. Many people don't realize their bodies are full of harmful toxins and that's what's causing them to feel bad. Most experts recommend you go through a deep cleansing where you put yourself on a fast and then eat a certain diet, staying away from things that are harmful. They say over time you'll rid yourself of those toxins and begin to feel better.

In the same way, there are all kinds of toxins that can build up in your mind. When you dwell on what you can't do and the hurts you've felt and the challenges you face, you are focusing on toxic thoughts that can do as much damage as toxins in your body.

Toxic thoughts build up and become like toxic waste that will eventually contaminate your whole life. They affect your attitude, your self-esteem, and your confidence. They become part of who you are. That's why the Scripture says in Proverbs that we should guard our heart because it affects all we do. Make guarding your mind a priority; put this at the top of your to-do list. If your mind is polluted, your whole life will be damaged.

You probably know someone who is bitter, cynical, and has a sour attitude. They expect the worst. Why is that? They've allowed toxic thoughts to take root. These negative thoughts are poisoning their future.

What's the solution? They need to go through a detoxification—not a physical cleansing but a mental cleansing. The only way they're going to be free, the only way they're going to get back to who God made them to be, is to detox the mind.

You may need to detox the bitterness, the low self-esteem, the negative words spoken over you, the condemnation from past mistakes, and the discouragement that's trying to become a part of you.

How do you detox? You make a decision that you're not going to dwell on those thoughts anymore. You starve those toxins. Every time you dwell on that negative thought, that condemnation, that bitterness, that low self-esteem, you are feeding it. You're giving it new life, making it stronger.

Those thoughts come saying, *You're never going to get well. You heard what the doctor said. You're never going to be happy. You've been hurt too many times. You're never going to accomplish your dreams.* But instead of dwelling on them, just say, "No, I'm not going there. I'm not dwelling on my hurt, or what I don't have, or my mistakes. I'm dwelling on what God says about me. He says I'm forgiven. He says He will pay me back double for every wrong. He says I am well able to fulfill my destiny. He says my best days are still in front of me."

If you ignore toxic thoughts and keep your mind filled with thoughts of hope, thoughts of faith, then those toxic thoughts will grow weaker, and before long they won't have any effect on you.

Today's Prayer

Father, today I choose to detox my mind and heart. I make it my top priority to renew my thoughts to Your Word. I declare that no longer will I meditate on negative, condemning thoughts but I will dwell on Your Word, which is truth that sets me free! In Jesus' Name. Amen.

Today's Thought

Make the decision today to detox any negative, self-defeating thoughts by meditating on God's promises instead. Detox bitterness, detox low self-esteem, detox negative words that may have been spoken over you, detox condemnation. Instead dwell on what God says about you. God says, "You are forgiven." God says, "Your best days are in front of you." God says, "I'll restore the years that the enemy has stolen." As you detox your mind and fill your thoughts with His promises, you'll see His hand of blessing on your life. You'll rise higher, and you'll live the abundant life He has for you.

You Are a Child of God

Scripture Reading: Galatians 3

You are all children of God through faith in Christ Jesus.

GALATIANS 3:26 NLT

I read about this young boy raised by a single mom in the hills of Tennessee. Back then, especially in that area, children born to unwed mothers were subject to extreme discrimination. In fact, when this boy was just three years old, the neighbors wouldn't allow him to play with their children. They said things like, "What's he doing in our town? And who is his father anyway?"

They treated him like he had some kind of plague. On Saturdays he would go with his mom to the local store and invariably people would make disparaging comments. They would say hurtful things loud enough on purpose so they could hear: "There they are again. Did you ever figure out who his dad is?"

This little boy grew up insecure, ridiculed, always feeling that there was something wrong with him. When the boy turned twelve, a new minister moved into the town. He was a young man, very gifted and very passionate. He created quite a stir. People were excited.

The boy had never been to church a day in his life, but one Sunday he decided to go hear a sermon by this new minister everybody was talking about. He got there late, snuck in, and sat toward the back so no one would notice him. As the boy listened that day, he felt a love and an acceptance that he had never felt before. He had planned to leave early, but he was so engrossed in what the minister was saying that the service was over before he knew it.

The boy was caught up in the crowd. As the young minister greeted everyone who was leaving, he saw the boy. He had never met him, and he didn't know anything about him. But the minister noticed the boy wasn't with anyone. He was by himself.

The minister said to him in a very friendly tone, "Young man, whose child are you?"

The room grew completely silent. The minister had asked the question everybody else wanted to ask. The boy didn't know what to say. He had heard all the talk that he was the outcast and a child with no dad. So he just put his head down.

The minister noticed something was wrong, something he obviously didn't know anything about. But God gave him wisdom. He was quick on his feet. He looked at the boy and said, "Oh, I know who your Father is. I can see the resemblance so strongly; why, you're a child of almighty God."

That day was a turning point in the boy's life. Those who had been talking about him put their heads down and walked out of the room. The stronghold of insecurity and inferiority was broken. He began to see himself not as the inferior outcast people said he was, but as a child of almighty God.

The boy went on to become very successful and live a blessed and happy life. Many people grow up without fathers. I wish it were not so, but if that's the case for you, let me tell you what the young minister told the boy. Your Father is almighty God. You have been chosen and set apart before the foundation of the world. You didn't get here by accident. You didn't just happen to show up. God breathed His life into you. He put seeds of greatness on the inside. You have a destiny to fulfill, an assignment, something that no one else can accomplish.

Today's Prayer

Father, thank You for making me your child through faith in Jesus Christ. Help me to see myself as royalty—the child of king—the way You see me. I release negative words spoken over me and receive Your love which renews and restores my soul. In Jesus' Name. Amen.

Today's Thought

Don't let what people say about you or what they don't say about you cause you to feel less than whole. Your earthly father may not be around as much as he should; maybe you don't even know him. But your heavenly Father says, "I am proud of you. You have a bright future. You're going to do great things."

Feed Your Mind God's Thoughts

Scripture Reading: Psalm 68

A father of the fatherless, and a judge of the widows, is God in his holy habitation.   PSALM 68:5 KJV

After the service a couple of years ago this young lady came up with two small children, a girl and a boy. They were so loving. The little boy hung on to me and didn't want to go. He was about five years old. I hugged him back and we talked for a little while and finally we high-fived and they walked away.

A couple of minutes later, the boy came back and said he wanted to whisper something in my ear. I leaned down, and I'll never forget what he said.

"I wish you were my dad."

That almost broke my heart. I told him what I'm telling you: Every morning, look up and just imagine your heavenly Father is smiling down on you. He's saying, "You're the apple of My eye. You're My most prized possession."

The Scripture says God will be a father to the fatherless. Many people are not reaching their full potential because of a lack of identity. Their minds are full of thoughts saying, *You're not from the right family,* or *You don't even have a father. No wonder you can't succeed.*

Don't believe those lies. Believe this instead: "I am who God says I am.

I may not have an earthly father, but I have a heavenly Father. People may have spoken negative things over me, but I know before anybody could curse me, God put a blessing on me. That's what I'm going to dwell on."

If you have had these negative things spoken over you and they are poisoning your future, go back to the roots of those thoughts. Who said you were not smart enough to go to college? Who said you would never be successful? Who told you that you don't have what it takes? Who said you would never be married? Who told you that you would never overcome this obstacle? Who said your best days are behind you?

I can promise you it was not God who put those thoughts in your mind. Detox that garbage. Detox what your ex-husband said about you. Detox what that teacher said you couldn't do. Detox what that manager said you would never become. Detox what those critics said about your ability.

Today's Prayer

Father, thank You for loving and setting me free. Thank You for being more than my God, for being my heavenly Father. You said I am the apple of Your eye. I receive your love today and every spiritual blessing You have for me. In Jesus' Name. Amen.

Today's Thought

Start a new diet today to clear out all the toxins. It will free you from all the negativity, all the *can't do it* thoughts, all the *not good enough* thoughts. This is faith food. When you eat this food, it's like Popeye eating spinach. It's like Clark Kent stepping into the phone booth and coming out Superman. A transformation takes place when you get rid of negative condemning thoughts and feed your mind what God says about you.

Treat the Root

Scripture Reading: Joshua 1

Study this Book of Instruction continually. Meditate on it day and night so you will be sure to obey everything written in it. Only then will you prosper and succeed in all you do. JOSHUA 1:8 NLT

We have a couple of pet rabbits at home, and a while back we noticed one of them looked like he wasn't feeling well. He kept rubbing the side of his face like something was bothering him. We checked it out and didn't see anything. He looked fine. A few days later that area had really swollen up. It looked like he had a big growth on his face.

So we took the rabbit to the vet. They gave him some antibiotics and said he should get better. We tried that for a week, but he didn't improve. In fact, he looked really bad. We took him back and they examined him again. This time they discovered the real problem was that a fly egg had somehow entered the rabbit's nasal passage. The fly larva was growing and about to hatch. That's why the rabbit's face was so infected.

No matter how many antibiotics the vet gave the rabbit, they didn't work. They had to get to the root of the problem. Once they found the source of the infection and removed it, the rabbit was fine.

This is the way the enemy works. He tries to plant these lies in your mind that infect your thinking. So often we deal with the surface problem and try to have a good attitude and a good self-image, but it's a constant struggle, like we're always going uphill.

Could you be like our vet and the rabbit, treating the symptoms but not dealing with the real issue? Are you treating the outside but missing the root cause, a negative mind-set toward yourself? Your thinking in some area may be infected.

Maybe you are trying to break an addiction, but deep down you still hear the words, *You'll be an alcoholic just like your father.* Maybe you are trying to make your marriage work but that thought keeps playing: *You'll get a divorce just like your parents.*

Those are lies, and they are infecting your thinking. The way to get rid of those thoughts is to meditate on what God says about you. The Scripture says to meditate on God's Word day and night. In other words, *continuously* have positive thoughts playing in your mind: *I am talented. I am creative. I am anointed. I am equipped. I am empowered. I am blessed. I am prosperous. I am disciplined. I am free from every addiction. I walk in divine health. I have the favor of God.*

Today's Prayer

Father, I invite You today to search my heart and mind. Show me where there are any roots of destruction in my life. Set me free once and for all from anything that would hold me back as I serve You with my whole heart. In Jesus' Name. Amen.

Today's Thought

I choose to have thoughts of faith, thoughts of hope, encouraging thoughts, and "can-do" thoughts to make me positive, hopeful, strong, and courageous.

Wear Your Blessings Well

Scripture Reading: Psalm 128

You will enjoy the fruit of your labor. How joyful and prosperous you will be. PSALM 128:3 NLT

A well-known reporter once referred to me as "the smiling preacher." That story caught on and went all over the world. But some people use that term in a derogatory sense, as in, "Why does he smile so much? What's wrong with him? He couldn't be that happy."

I was young and new to the ministry, and at first I thought, *Well, maybe I shouldn't smile so much. People are making fun.* Then I realized I don't have to hide God's blessings. I don't have to apologize because I smile all the time. I'm wearing my blessings well.

When you keep God in first place and do your best to honor Him, the Scripture says, God's blessings will chase you down and overtake you. That means you will come into happiness, increase, promotion, and good breaks, even some that you didn't necessarily deserve. That's God rewarding you for walking in His ways.

We see this principle in the Old Testament with Ruth. She was out in the fields following behind the workers and gathering up the leftover wheat they had missed.

One day the owner of the fields, Boaz, told those workers to leave handfuls of wheat on purpose for Ruth. Now Ruth didn't have to struggle any-more. She didn't have to work night and day. Ruth came into blessings that were simply dropped at her feet.

Today's Prayer

Father, thank You for your handfuls on purpose—Your blessings and favor that I didn't work for. Thank You for setting me in the right place at the right time with the right people to fulfill the destiny You have in store for me. In Jesus' Name. Amen.

Today's Thought

Every one of us can look back and see times where God has left us handfuls of blessing on purpose, something that we didn't deserve, that we didn't have to struggle for, that we didn't even ask for. We just stumbled into it. Now here is my challenge: Don't apologize for God's goodness. Don't downplay what God has done in your life. Don't make excuses because a friend might be jealous. Don't try to hide God's blessings because a coworker might judge you and think that it's not fair.

Favor Is Not Always Fair

Scripture Reading: Psalm 118

The LORD has done this, and it is marvelous in our eyes. The LORD has done it this very day; let us rejoice today and be glad.

PSALM 118:23–24 NIV

We used to sing a song growing up called "Look What the Lord Has Done." When you go around on God's goodness, when you're giving Him all the credit, you are wearing your blessings well.

David said, "The LORD has done this, and it is marvelous in our eyes." That is a great attitude. Give God credit for every good thing that happens: "This is the Lord's doing."

"You know what our new building is? It's the Lord's doing."

"My mother is still enjoying life thirty years after being diagnosed with terminal cancer. You know what that is? That's the Lord's doing. It's marvelous in our eyes."

If you always see the promotion, the good break, the healing, the new, and the opportunities coming your way as the Lord's doing, you won't have any problem wearing your blessings well.

I used to feel kind of guilty that God has given me such a great life. I've always been happy and blessed to have great parents and grandparents, a beautiful wife, and wonderful children. Again and again Victoria and I have seen these handfuls of blessings on purpose.

We've just been blessed, and it's the Lord's doing. But when I used to see people dealing with hardships and struggling to overcome them, I tried to downplay how God has blessed me so they wouldn't feel bad. But I've learned that doesn't bring any honor to God. God wants us to be examples of His goodness. I don't have to apologize if I get a handful of blessings on purpose and somebody else doesn't. You don't either; we are supposed to wear our blessings well.

Today's Prayer

Father, thank You for Your favor and blessing in my life. I choose to wear my blessing well. I choose to glorify You for the good things You have done for me. Let my life be a testimony of Your faithfulness. In Jesus' Name. Amen.

Today's Thought

You may not feel you deserved a blessing, but favor is not always fair. It's just the goodness of God. The moment you start apologizing for what God has done and downplaying His goodness, God will find somebody else to favor. I'm not saying show off and brag on what you have and how great you are. But brag on how great God is.

Promotion Comes from the Lord

Scripture Reading: Ephesians 3

To him who is able to do immeasurably more than all we ask or imagine, according to his power that is at work within us, to him be glory.
EPHESIANS 3:20–21 NIV

A young man in our congregation came to me after he was promoted to a high position at a major retail company. He was the youngest ever to hold the job overseeing a large region. He was very excited. He knew it was God's favor.

But he was promoted over coworkers who had been there much longer and were more experienced. They had been his friends, but he felt they were avoiding him since his promotion. He sensed that they were trying to make him look bad by talking about him behind his back.

"I know you've quoted Ephesians 3:20 in situations like this," he said to me. "This is just what you've been talking about, but I feel guilty, like I've done something wrong."

I told him what I'm telling you: That is the goodness of God. Wear it well. The Scripture tells us that promotion doesn't come from people; promotion comes from the Lord (see Psalm 75:6–7).

If you don't step up and wear that blessing well with a grateful attitude, do you know what will happen? God will give it to somebody else! Don't worry if others are jealous or turn against you. I've learned some people will be your friend until you get promoted. Coworkers may go to lunch with you as long as you're at the same level, but the moment you see increase, the moment you come into a handful of blessings on purpose, jealousy takes hold and they try to make you look bad. Don't worry about it. God will take care of your enemies. Be grateful for the goodness of God.

We see an example of this in the Scripture when Isaac was in a famine. There had been a great drought in the land for some time. It didn't look like there was any end in sight. Isaac went out to his land and he planted crops, right in the middle of the famine. It didn't make any sense, but somehow in that same year, without the proper amount of water, Isaac received one hundred times what he had sown because the Lord blessed him (see Genesis 26:12).

Notice where the blessing came from: almighty God. It was a handful of blessings on purpose; supernatural increase. But what's interesting is that when Isaac's crops came up, when God blessed him, the people he was living around, the Philistines, his friends, all of a sudden became jealous of him.

They were fine as long as Isaac was hungry, too. As long as they were at the same level, it was no big deal, but when he stepped up to a new level, when he began to wear his blessings well, the Scripture says, "the Philistines envied Isaac" (Genesis 26:14 NIV).

Today's Prayer

Father, thank You for promotion in my life. Thank You for increase. Thank You for abundance. Thank You for blessing me because You are good and Your mercy endures forever. I choose to wear my blessing well and bring glory to You. In Jesus' Name. Amen.

Today's Thought

So often we think, *Is it wrong for me to want to live in a nice house? Is it wrong for me to want a bigger piece of property? Is it selfish for*

me to want to drive a nice car? Is it okay for me to want to bless my
children and leave them an inheritance?

God says, "It's okay. Wear your blessings well." As long as
you're keeping God in first place and you're not living selfishly
and you're not making material things your idols, then God
wants to give you the desires of your heart. He takes pleasure in
blessing His children.

Don't Apologize for God's Goodness

Scripture Reading: Deuteronomy 28

All these blessings will come on you and accompany you if you obey the
Lord your God.   DEUTERONOMY 28:2 NIV

My parents sowed seeds for forty years before I ever took over the
Lakewood ministry. I'm reaping the rewards of a generational blessing.
My paternal grandmother made ten cents an hour washing clothes for
other people during the Great Depression. She worked twelve hours a day
and made $1.20. My father went to school with holes in his pants. He
would put cardboard in the bottom of his shoes because the soles were so
torn up.

My grandparents and parents made great sacrifices to get us where we
are today. So I'm wearing my blessings well. People may criticize us. They
may judge. They may find fault, but they don't know what it took to get
where we are today.

They weren't there when the kids in our family would sweep out the
old church and clean buildings. They weren't there when my father traveled for weeks doing missionary work around the world while my mother
took care of five children on her own. They weren't there when my mom
was diagnosed with terminal cancer and we fought the good fight of faith.
They weren't there when my father went to be with the Lord and I stepped
up to pastor the church practically scared to death.

Some people come in after the struggle and they see you as you are now: blessed, prosperous, healthy, sober, free, and happy. They want to judge you and criticize, but the problem is, they missed seeing the years of struggle. They didn't see the sacrifices made. They didn't see the battles fought—the times you felt like giving up but you kept pressing forward, the nights you stayed up and prayed and believed and gave and served. They didn't see the price that was paid to get you to where you are.

A blessing may look free, but the truth is, it cost you something. Ruth's blessing, her handful on purpose, came after she had buried her husband and after her father-in-law had died. She had suffered great heartache and pain.

I'm sure some of those workers said, "Hey, it's not fair. Why is this lady getting all this free wheat when we have to work?" They didn't realize Ruth had paid the price. She had proven herself as being faithful. She was taking care of her loved ones. God was rewarding her.

Today's Prayer

Father, thank You for Your goodness and faithfulness in my life. I declare that I will not hide my blessing, I will not apologize for Your goodness but I will bless and praise You for it. Help me to be an example of Your love as I wear my blessing well. In Jesus' Name. Amen.

Today's Thought

When you wear a blessing well and you take one of those handfuls of blessing on purpose, don't be surprised if it draws jealousy out of people. When they come at you, simply say, in a humble way, "I'm wearing this blessing well, despite criticism and jealousy. If my friends aren't happy for my blessings, then it's time to find new friends who will celebrate with me as I celebrate with them."